Y 385 AUL

"ALL ABOARD!"

THE STORY OF PASSENGER TRAINS IN AMERICA

Phil Ault

ILLUSTRATED WITH PHOTOGRAPHS AND OLD PRINTS

DODD, MEAD & COMPANY
New York

Library of Congress Cataloging in Publication Data

Ault, Phillip H   date
    "All aboard!"
    Bibliography: p.

    Includes index.
    SUMMARY: Traces the history of the passenger train
in the United States. Anecdotes describe travel on a
number of well-known runs.
    1.   Railroads—United States—Passenger traffic—
Juvenile literature.   [1.   Railroads—Passenger traffic]
I.   Title.
HE2583.A84   385'.22'0973   76-12505
ISBN 0-396-07350-6

*To the memory of my father, who commuted by
train daily for more than fifty years*

CONTENTS

Santa Fe's El Capitan rounds a curve in California.

1

RIDING THE CENTURY

America grew up to the siren call of the steam locomotive whistle. Under the feathery touch of engineers who played them almost like musical instruments, the whistles of a thousand passenger-train locomotives rushing along the tracks under black clouds of coal smoke somehow sounded insistent, mournful, stimulating, and lonesome, all at once. They beckoned to distant places in a day when the United States still had a frontier to be explored and the train was the only fast way of getting there.

To boys and girls in small towns, the long, doleful whistle blast of a passenger train rolling across the countryside at night was a summons to adventure. Dreaming, they wondered what it would be like to be going toward the big city on that train. From what they had read in books, they tried to visualize how it would be, hurtling along on a luxury train instead of plodding to the next town on a dirt road behind the family horse. Those who were young just after the year 1900 dreamed more than anything about riding on the most wondrous, thrilling train of all, the new Twentieth Century Limited.

Of all the trains the United States has known, the Century was the most famous. Aboard its Pullmans on the high-speed run between New York and Chicago rode the wealthy and the renowned. Presidents of the United States appeared on its passenger lists, along with stage and motion picture stars, eminent

1

men of business, and foreign princesses. Up front, behind the thundering locomotive, the Railway Mail Service car carried millions of dollars in securities between the financial markets of the country's two largest cities.

Who, then, could have believed that some day the Twentieth Century Limited would disappear and become only a memory, along with hundreds of lesser passenger trains that have been forced out of existence by competition from the airplane and the automobile? The airplane hadn't even been invented when the first run of the Century was made on June 15, 1902. Automobiles were only sputtering, chugging horseless carriages owned as playthings by a handful of rich men.

Even thirty years later, nobody among the finely dressed men and women who boarded the Century in Chicago one sunny spring afternoon in 1935 for the overnight trip to New York would have thought such a fate conceivable. Although small, two-motored commercial airliners had begun restricted service between some cities, the Century was regarded as the ultimate word in swift, luxurious travel—961 miles from La Salle Street Station in downtown Chicago to Grand Central Terminal in the heart of Manhattan in seventeen hours. Passengers paid extra fare to ride the Century and considered the special facilities of the train worth every penny of it.

Arriving at the Chicago terminal, a passenger stepped from his taxicab to find a Redcap porter at his side with a two-wheeled cart, ready to trundle the baggage from curbside to his train. Overhead an "L" train on Chicago's elevated electric commuter railroad line rumbled past, showering sparks from its brakes.

"To the Century. Car 130," the traveler said. "I want this bag at the seat with me. Check the rest of them, please."

The Redcap hurried into the station, pushing his load. The passenger followed more slowly, topcoat over his arm, the brim of his felt hat snapped down in front with a hint of jauntiness. He wouldn't have thought of traveling to New York bareheaded. Especially not on the Century. Looking at his wristwatch, he saw that he still had twenty minutes to train time. There was no great hurry.

2

Old print shows busy Chicago railway center.

Yet, as he entered the cavernous, marble-floored La Salle Street Station, he found himself walking faster. Anticipation stirred him, no matter how casual he tried to be. At the news stand he put down two cents for an early afternoon edition of the Chicago *Daily News*, glancing at the front page headlines as he approached the train gate.

A row of black iron folding gates divided the high-ceilinged waiting room from the train shed. At an open gate, a uniformed trainman with gold braid and a brass badge on his cap checked the tickets of passengers passing through. Above his head, white letters on a black sign announced:

> No. 26
> The Twentieth Century Limited
> New York
> Departs 2:00

Showing his ticket to the gateman, the traveler stepped through the gate onto a red carpet. This had been unrolled along the platform ahead, the entire length of the train which stood on the adjoining track. Red carpet service—that was the Century. Let those who rode on the less important trains lined up at nearby platforms walk on bare concrete, but Century passengers deserved special footing.

His attention was caught by the popping flashbulbs of news photographers aiming their Graflex cameras at the rear of the

3

Well-dressed women wait on observation platform of the Twentieth Century Limited as famous train prepares for departure.

train. A beautiful, smiling woman, the fur collar of her spring coat drawn close around her shoulders, posed on the open platform of the observation car. She was obscured from the waist down by a round electric sign, "20th Century Limited," that hung from a gleaming brass rail. In spite of himself, the passenger felt a tingle of thrill as he recognized her. Of course he should know her, after seeing her on the movie screen so often. Seated by a window in the car, talking into the telephone that connected the

Century with the rest of the world until a moment before its departure, was a familiar film hero. Riding the Century and posing for pictures on it was part of the glamour treatment Hollywood studios gave their stars.

A small "130" identified the traveler's Pullman among the line of dark green cars along which he walked. At the door he saw a Pullman porter in high-necked, starched white jacket and his own Redcap. The Redcap handed him the checks for his unneeded baggage so he could reclaim the bags when he left the train in Grand Central Station tomorrow morning. He dropped a tip into the man's partially outstretched hand.

"Lower 8," he told the Pullman porter.

"To your right, sir."

Entering the Pullman, the traveler walked along a narrow corridor, past wide windows on one side and metal doors marked by discreet initials on the other. These were the drawing rooms, bedrooms and compartments, larger, secluded accommodations more expensive than the lower berth he had purchased. The narrow side corridor curved to the middle of the car, after passing the

A Santa Fe Pullman section of the Thirties

last bedroom, and broadened into a central aisle that was bordered on either side by high-backed green upholstered seats. Lower 8 awaited him, along with his suitcase put aboard by the Redcap.

He settled back in the seat and watched passengers hurrying along the red carpet. A glance at his watch; it was almost time to leave. Another passenger, breathing heavily from hurrying, sat down on the seat facing him. This was "Upper 8," the man who would sleep that night above his head in the upper berth, now folded back on its hinges and locked in place so it looked like part of the Pullman's curving upper wall.

As he turned to the window again the passenger thought that the train on the adjoining track had begun to move backward. The platform seemed to, also. In fact, the Century had started forward—no jerk, no roaring of motors, just a soft gliding movement.

"We're on our way," he said to his seatmate.

The passengers aboard the Twentieth Century Limited had been taken under the charge of steam railroading's finest, fastest operation. Until they stepped onto the platform at Grand Central seventeen hours later, they were held in a luxurious steel cocoon, moving across the earth but feeling as though they were separated from it.

Precisely at 2:00 P.M., the conductor at the open door of the observation car had looked at the gold watch in his right hand, called "All aboard!" and waved his left arm to the engineer who

This huge locomotive was overhauled and streamlined in 1939 to pull the Twentieth Century Limited, before diesel locomotives were used.

was leaning from his locomotive cab nearly a quarter mile away at the head of the sixteen-car train. The engineer inched open the throttle, the conductor swung aboard the observation car, and the train began to gather momentum.

Sixty-six men and women would do their jobs aboard the Century by the time it pulled into Grand Central the next morning, some making the train go, others tending to the desires of the passengers—a far larger staff than would be needed by the giant jet airliners of the future to zoom across the continent. Eight crews of engineers and firemen would take turns in the locomotive. Conductors, baggagemen, porters, a crew of twenty-four cooks and waiters in the two dining cars, brakemen, and, for the extra convenience of the passengers, a barber, a maid, a tailor, and a public stenographer had roles in making the Century function.

The train was pulled by a single giant steam locomotive weighing 182 tons, so powerful that it hauled the long string of cars at more than eighty miles an hour. In the moments before departure time, the fireman had oiled the towering drive wheels with a long-spouted can. Hissing steam hinted at the pent-up power about to be unleashed. Bell tolling, the locomotive poured billows of white steam from its stack as it set to its task. Every fifteen minutes along the route the roaring fire in its boiler would gulp a ton of coal. The sixteen thousand gallons of water stored in its tender behind the locomotive as it left Chicago would be swallowed and converted to steam so swiftly that the water in the tanks had to be

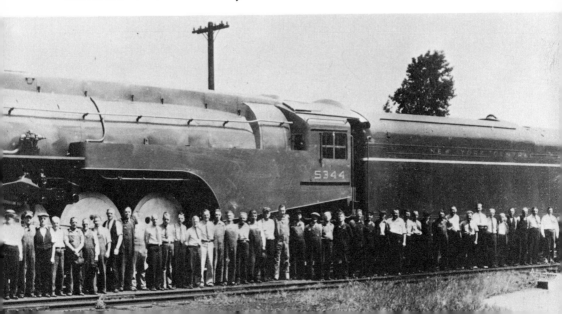

replenished frequently, on the run.

The Century couldn't afford the time to stop for water, so it refilled its tank at high speed. At intervals along the New York Central route, long shallow pans of water were placed between the rails. Slowing the train momentarily to about sixty miles an hour, the locomotive crew lowered a scoop under the engine so that it dipped into the long tank and sucked up the water into the tender. Delicate timing was required. If the scoop wasn't pulled up in time, too much water was taken aboard and the tank on the tender overflowed. To prevent a miscalculation that might overload the tank and rupture it, a large square hole was cut in the top of the storage tank at its rear, just ahead of the baggage car.

In the early days of the Twentieth Century Limited, on one trip the scoop wasn't pulled up in time. Water gushed out of the overflow hole so hard that it burst open the front door of the baggage car. The water poured through the baggage compartment. Into the barber shop it rolled, sending the startled barber scurrying back into the smoking compartment with the foaming water at his heels. After that, the forward doors of Century baggage cars were bolted shut.

Veteran Century trainmen had a favorite yarn about a hobo who sneaked a free ride by perching himself on the front of the baggage car, just behind the locomotive tender. Possibly the locomotive fireman saw him, possibly not. Perhaps it was just a coincidence that twice on that run the fireman waited too long to pull up the scoop, so the overflow water splashed against the front of the baggage car. When the train halted for a change of engine crews, the drenched hobo climbed down from his precarious perch and asked the engineer, "What was the names of them two rivers we ran through back there?"

When the New York Central introduced the Twentieth Century Limited between New York and Chicago soon after the start of the new century, the train was intended to exhibit the spectacular leaps forward that the railroad industry was making. It was a time of optimism. The inventions that had crowded upon the heels of each other during the last quarter of the 1800's were

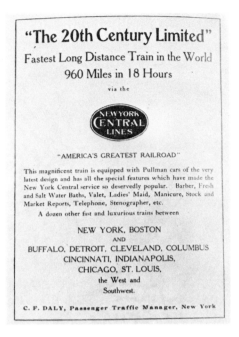

Ad published about 1910 describes the luxurious facilities provided aboard the Twentieth Century Limited.

being refined and improved. Americans, or at least those who could afford to, were beginning to enjoy the luxuries that their expanding industrial might was producing.

That was the intent behind creation of the Twentieth Century Limited, to make it a showpiece of American mechanical luxury, the finest of everything on wheels designed for those who would and could pay the price. Extra touches were added, such as a Christmas tree in the club car during the holiday season. All the Century's passenger cars were Pullman sleepers; there was no place on this train for the traveler who wanted to save money by sitting up all night on a daycoach.

Originally the Century operated on a twenty-hour schedule. After three years this was reduced to eighteen hours. In the spring of 1935, with the addition of even more powerful locomotives, the time between the two cities was trimmed again, to seventeen hours. To meet such a demanding schedule, the king of the New York Central's vast system of rails must have the highball sign—full speed ahead—every mile of the way. Everything else must give way.

9

2

SWIFTLY THROUGH THE NIGHT

Back in the Pullman cars of the Century, the passengers settled down for the trip, talking, reading, watching the scenery. Some asked the porters to set up tables between the facing seats so they could play cards. With gathering speed as the train drew free from Chicago, the *clickety-click* sound of the steel wheels rolling over switches and cross tracks turned into a rhythmic *clack-clack-clack*. All signal lights ahead were green. Heavy as they were, the Pullmans rocked slightly. Cinders from the trailing smoke of the locomotive snapped occasionally against the windows, despite metal baffles set at an angle outside each pane to divert them.

The passenger in Lower 8 walked back to the club car; that was one of the pleasures of train travel, the freedom to roam about. Settling into one of the swiveled lounge chairs, he read a magazine and was sipping a drink brought by the porter when the Century's pace slowed. After a hundred-mile dash across flat northern Indiana, the train stopped at Elkhart to change engine crews. A secretary came aboard and distributed sheets in the club car listing the closing prices on that day's New York Stock Exchange, received by telegraph at Elkhart. To many businessmen, the figures on the sheets were important news, meaning profits or losses on their investments. Important business deals at the opening of tomorrow morning's New York stock market would be decided aboard the Century that night, based on these sheets of

figures. The businessmen didn't want to wait for the facts until they could buy a New York newspaper the next morning.

With the train rolling again, Mr. Lower 8 strolled to the observation car at the rear of the train, squeezing past oncoming passengers in the narrow corridors at the ends of the Pullmans. His intention was to sit outside on the observation platform, in one of the half-dozen chairs beneath the overhanging awning. He was afraid that the chairs would be filled, but they weren't. Seating

Above: *First and second sections of the Twentieth Century Limited confer during brief stop at Elkhart, Indiana, in 1928.*

Right: *Observation car on the Santa Fe Scout*

himself, he watched as the tracks receded behind the speeding train, the rails drawing closer and closer together in the distance until they merged on the horizon—a splendid demonstration of perspective, an art teacher would call it.

At every mile, a small post at trackside showed the distance from Chicago. He remembered a trick somebody had taught him about telling how fast a train was moving. Each time a car wheel passed over a joint in the rails, it made a click. The number of clicks heard in a span of twenty seconds was almost exactly the miles per hour the train was going. Counting intently while checking his wristwatch, he discovered that the Century was rolling across western Ohio well above eighty miles an hour.

A burning sensation stung his left eye. Another flicked his cheek. Cinders! He realized now why nobody was occupying the chairs. Exciting as it looked, the observation platform was no place to be when the train was rolling at such speed.

Twilight was falling. As the Century swung around a curve, his eyes followed the long horizontal streak of light from the Pullman windows which cut a swath through the gathering darkness. He decided it was time for dinner.

Making his way forward to the entrance to the twin dining cars, he was greeted by an elegant headwaiter in striped trousers, a white carnation adorning the buttonhole of his black coat.

"This way, sir." Rows of tables for four, covered by gleaming white cloths that fell almost to the carpeted floor, lined the broad windows on each side of the diner. A cut glass vase of fresh flowers decorated each table. Starched napkins folded into pyramids stood between the cutlery at each place.

The steward handed him a menu, an order ticket, and a pencil. Dinner was $1.35 for several courses starting with the Century's special watermelon pickles, followed by steak and dessert, served with a flourish by a waiter in white jacket and long white apron. Orders for dinner were not given orally in a dining car. To avoid confusion, the passenger wrote his selections on the ticket, which his waiter passed to the cooks in the narrow, compact galley at the end of the car.

Watching these cooks at work, if you were able to peek into

Dining car cooks work closely together in small kitchens while their trains travel at high speeds.

their cramped quarters, was a treat. With little space in which to move, they produced elaborate entrees, making use of every spare inch. From the galley came a parade of dinners, carried by the waiters on trays with each course covered by a silver lid. Because the aisle between the tables was narrow, and the waiters had to squeeze past each other, they balanced the trays above their heads at a seemingly precarious angle. But few passengers ever saw a morsel of food dropped.

At high speeds, the Century dining car rocked at times when the track was a little rough. This wasn't quite like eating in the family dining room. The waiters when pouring coffee filled the cups only halfway. Water occasionally sloshed back and forth in the carafes on the table. Yet even long-experienced travelers had a sense of stimulation at dining so luxuriously while outside the window the countryside raced past. They felt like special people, detached from the everyday world.

At the end of the meal, as an extra touch of elegance, the waiter placed a silver finger bowl filled with water on the table. The diner dipped his fingers into the bowl to remove any crumbs or grease from the meal, then wiped them on his napkin. On one trip on the Century, the small son of this writer, having a finger bowl placed before him and not having been instructed in its use, startled the dining car waiter and embarrassed his family by picking it up and drinking the water.

Making his way back to Car 130 after dinner, the passenger discovered that he was entering new surroundings. While the occupants were dining or chatting in the club car, the Pullman porter had made up the car for the night. He had pulled down each upper berth from its hinged, concealed location and made up both lower and upper berth beds. The lower berth was formed by sliding down the backs of the seats to form a solid bridge across the daytime leg space. Portable metal partitions had been slid into place to separate the sections. At each berth a small hinged ladder was attached, up which the upper-berth sleeper climbed to his bed.

Heavy green curtains were drawn across every berth, so that walking through the Pullman was like going through a narrow, cloth-lined canyon. What had been an open car in daytime, where passengers could see each other, had become a double line of private cubicles.

After washing and brushing his teeth in the men's lounge at the end of the car, the passenger in Lower 8 stepped through the curtained opening of his berth and undressed, his body forming a curtain-covered bulge in the aisle. Other passengers accidentally bumped him through the curtain as they passed, especially when he leaned down to remove his shoes. A Pullman car at going-to-bed time was a peculiar kind of close-packed privacy. The passenger's smaller items he placed in a green net hammock swinging gently along the outside wall of his berth. His coat and trousers went onto a hanger attached to the webbing inside the

14

Note the upper berths in the ceiling, which were pulled down at night on the old Pullmans. Interior of the Santa Fe Scout.

aisle curtains. He slipped his shoes slightly out into the aisle, knowing that the porter would collect them during the night and shine them. Then, crawling under the covers, he settled down to read with light from a small lamp behind his head.

Going to bed in a Pullman berth wasn't easy, but once into bed the passenger had a sense of cosiness and of being in a private niche of his own. Forgetting that he was surrounded by others— and with another sleeper over his head—came easily enough, except when someone nearby began to snore. Even the muffling effect of the heavy green curtains wasn't enough to block that penetrating *snuugh–snuugh* sound.

Later, turning off the berth light, the passenger raised the window shade a few inches. Propped on one elbow, he peered into the darkness, sprinkled by lights from farmhouses. Then, without warning, came the shattering brightness of clustered lights, a momentary glimpse of a railroad station, the red and green gleam of store signs, the headlights of automobiles lined up beyond the lowered crossing gates—the Century had steamed full speed through a city without breaking its pace.

Through the night the Century thundered, never stopping for passengers, occasionally only for changes of train crews. In the middle of the night at Cleveland, a new locomotive replaced the original one. The train sped on through eastern Ohio and a corner of Pennsylvania, then along the shore of Lake Erie to Buffalo, New York, and eastward across the Empire State toward Albany.

In fact, sleep did not come easily to some passengers, especially those more than six feet tall who found their beds slightly shorter than they wished them to be. The motion of the train, the constant *clack-clack* of the wheels, the mournful whistle of the locomotive, the sense of being on the move, kept many of them from falling asleep immediately. Those in the more cramped but cheaper upper berths were affected especially. The restlessness of travel fever strikes even the most experienced.

At 6:30 A.M., the time he had requested, the man in Lower 8 sensed a discreet shaking of the curtains. The porter said softly, "It's six-thirty, sir. We're past Albany." Dressing quickly, the pas-

Twentieth Century Limited races along New York Central tracks, 1909. At Croton-Harmon, locomotives are still replaced by electric engines which take trains into New York City.

senger went to the men's lounge at the end of the car to wash and shave. Refreshed, he hurried through the club car, picked up a New York morning newspaper that had been put aboard at the last service stop, and went in to breakfast.

He was fortunate; a window seat on the right side of the diner was available, providing a beautiful view of the Hudson River flowing close to the tracks. The ride from Albany to New York City down the east bank of the Hudson is among the most scenic on all American railroads. As he was finishing his corn sticks, a special delicacy of the train, and his coffee, the Century slowed to a stop. "Harmon," his waiter reported. "We're right on time."

Up front, the steam locomotive was uncoupled and diverted onto a siding. In its place, an electric locomotive was hooked onto the train for the final run into Manhattan. This was necessary because in upper Manhattan the New York Central tracks entered a long tunnel under the city into Grand Central Terminal. Steam locomotives could not be used in the tunnel; the billows of smoke they exhaled would have smothered trainmen and passengers.

With their journey almost ended, the passengers returned to their Pullman spaces to assemble coats and hand luggage. Instantly at 96th Street, the daylight disappeared. The train rolled ahead through the tunnel under Park Avenue, its engineer guided through the gloom by the green electric "go" signals at the edge of the track. Above their heads, midtown Manhattan's morning automobile and trolley traffic jam grew. The first of the day's workers streamed into the skyscrapers.

At 57th Street the man in the underground "tower" alongside the track flashed word ahead by telephone that the Century was pulling in. Switch tenders in the terminal's main control tower pulled the proper handles. The headlight of the train beaming through the darkness, a few moments later the Century *clickety-clacked* across the switches and onto the designated arrival track.

Word of its approach also had been signaled to the Redcap waiting area in Grand Central Terminal. Dozens of porters raced down the concrete slope of the arrival platform, anxious to grab the suitcases of arriving passengers. The long train slid to a stop as gently as it had pulled out of Chicago. Their white jackets

17

Barefoot boys watch as the Twentieth Century Limited pauses briefly at Elkhart, Indiana, in 1913. Notice the train's name on the awning above the observation car "porch" on this old postcard.

buttoned to the neck, the Pullman porters opened the doors of their cars and gently handed each of the passengers out onto the platform. Always they managed to have one hand free to accept the generous tips they knew they could expect.

The Twentieth Century Limited had arrived—on time, proud symbol of the kind of railroading that had helped to build the United States, yet destined to disappear in a changing world which within a surprisingly few years would see supersonic jet planes spanning the oceans and men walking on the moon. Steam railroading would become only a memory kept alive by a few excursion trains crowded with summer vacationers—trains that at best could only give a hint of the glories of the Century.

3

TOM THUMB RACES A HORSE

The snorting steel giants that pulled the Twentieth Century Limited had an ancestor named *Tom Thumb*. This perky little steam kettle on wheels puffed its way into the history books not only because it was the first American-built locomotive to pull a passenger coach but because it raced against a horse—and lost.

Businessmen in the cities of the young United States around 1825 began hearing about a new kind of transportation being tried in England, called a railroad. Among those who decided to experiment with railroads in this country were men in Baltimore, Maryland. These men saw the need for better transportation from their Atlantic Ocean port city to the Ohio River, and then to the newly developing Ohio and Indiana country beyond. The only way to move people and goods at that time was by wagon over miserable, rutted mud tracks that passed for roads.

Thus the Baltimore and Ohio Railroad was born. Ground was broken for it on a farm at the edge of Baltimore on July 4, 1828. On that memorable day, the first ceremonial shovelful of dirt was turned by Charles Carroll of Carrollton. Ninety years old and growing feeble, Carroll was the only survivor of the men who had signed the Declaration of Independence in 1776, fifty-two years earlier. Thus he became a symbol, spanning the heroic Revolutionary War days of America and the start of the country's industrial era.

Old print shows Cincinnati in 1810, reached by flatboat and Conestoga wagons. Later it became a rail center.

Red, white, and blue bunting festooned the speakers' platform. Bands played a march composed in Carroll's honor. The audience bared their heads while a speaker read the Declaration of Independence. As the cornerstone of the railroad was being tapped into place, the aged patriot said to a friend, "I consider this

20

among the most important acts of my life, second only to my signing of the Declaration of Independence, if second even to that. . . ."

Soon the Baltimore and Ohio had a double line of tracks laid thirteen miles to a small community called Endicotts Mills. These tracks were narrow lengths of wood on which thin straps of iron were nailed, to give the top of the rail a harder riding surface. Called "snakeheads," these iron strips on early railroads had a vicious way of coming unfastened at one end, then curling up and stabbing through the floor of passenger coaches. Occasionally a passenger was killed in this manner.

Double-decked passenger coaches, replicas of those used on the Baltimore and Ohio Railroad in 1832

Passenger coaches built for the first railroad looked like over-sized stagecoaches placed on platforms, with four wheels underneath. Unlike those on stagecoaches, these wheels were of iron and had flanges on the inside to keep them from slipping off the rail, a precaution that often was insufficient to prevent derailments. On top of the stagecoach part, a second deck was built, with an awning to give slight protection to rooftop passengers seated on a long bench. These coaches looked top heavy, and were. Altogether, thirty-six men in high hats and women in long cumbersome gowns could be crowded into one of these cars, a few of the men being required to stand.

Riding the railroad coaches thirteen miles out to Endicotts Mills became the rage of Baltimore. Crowds stood in line for tickets every day to enjoy the thrill of rolling along smoothly—and to them, swiftly—over the tracks. The lines of passenger carriages were called not trains but "brigades of cars."

In truth, the passengers perched high on the B & O cars faced little danger either of being thrown overboard by the vibration of the speeding train or of getting cinders in their eyes. The trains moved only as fast as a horse could trot, or walk, which usually was the case, because horses were the motive power that pulled the first American trains.

Two years after the B & O began, in 1830, something exciting happened to change all that.

Visitors from England reported that in their country, railroads were experimenting with steam engines to pull trains. American engineers who made the tedious sailing-ship voyage to England to examine these locomotives returned with the bad news that the engines did nicely on the straight tracks common in England but couldn't pull a train around a sharp curve. Even the thirteen-mile stretch of B & O track had such curves.

Among those interested in the B & O was Peter Cooper, a renowned New York merchant with investments in Baltimore. Cooper hid the heart of an inventor beneath the formal clothing and dignity of an affluent businessman.

"I think I can knock together a locomotive that can get our trains around those curves," he told the railroad directors.

The steam engine he built was not much longer than those little handcars on which track workers scoot along railroads today. As Cooper described it later, the locomotive's boiler wasn't much bigger than a washboiler women used on laundry day. Tubes for the boiler were made from the barrels of muskets, from which Cooper had broken off the wooden parts. The steam produced by the upright boiler was harnessed to the wheels, providing the power to turn them. Cooper named the machine *Tom Thumb*, because it was so small.

Tom Thumb's moment of glory arrived when Cooper invited directors of the railroad to ride on a coach drawn by his locomotive from Baltimore to Endicotts Mills and back. Cooper himself ran the locomotive.

The guests were in party mood in splendid weather, shouting and laughing at the novel experience. Around the shortest of the curves *Tom Thumb* puffed with its passenger coach at an

This replica of the famous pioneer locomotive Tom Thumb *shows what a small machine it was.*

PETER COOPER'S "TOM THUMB" 1829-30 BALTIMORE & OHIO R. R.

astounding fifteen miles an hour. Even faster it went, up to eighteen miles an hour! At this breakneck speed, some of the men drew memorandum pads from their coat pockets and wrote messages in them, to prove that steadiness of hand was possible on a railroad even at such a pace.

Triumph turned to embarrassment on the way home, however.

At a point eight miles from Baltimore called Relay House, where the horses that normally pulled the railroad cars were changed, a powerful gray horse had been harnessed to a passenger coach on the second track. A stagecoach company had challenged Tom Thumb to a race back into the city, a challenge that the confident Cooper had accepted readily. Here was an opportunity for him to show how this new steam power would force the horses right out to pasture.

At the starting signal, the horse-drawn train took the lead; *Tom Thumb*'s little steam boiler needed time to get up momentum. The horse was nearly a quarter of a mile ahead when the brave but flimsy locomotive got rolling in its best style.

As they moved along the parallel tracks, the *Tom Thumb* overtook the horse. The railroad directors in the passenger car cheered lustily as the steam engine drew ahead. Victory to modern machinery! Ah, but not quite. *Tom Thumb* was widening the lead when calamity struck. A pulley attached to the locomotive's wheels operated the blower that forced a draught through the boiler. This pulley slipped off its drum and the engine lost power. Cooper cut his hands as he tried to tug the pulley back into place. Up came the horse from the rear and trotted past the exasperated inventor while he wrestled to correct the breakdown. By the time Cooper had *Tom Thumb* breathing steam again, the horse-drawn train was too far in front to be caught, arriving in Baltimore well ahead.

Victory for the horse made the stagecoach operators gloat, but it was the last success they ever could claim over the steam railroads. Other animals had tussles with the new steam-snorting vehicles, too. In Pennsylvania, an angry Durham bull charged an oncoming locomotive, and lost. Cows browsed on the tracks so frequently that cowcatchers had to be built on the fronts of loco-

The first American trains were drawn by horses. This painting by H. D. Stitt depicts changing horses at a relay station.

The first steam train used on the Mohawk and Hudson Railroad in New York State, 1831. A "car" on the same line.

motives to shove the bovine creatures out of the way.

Even though they were prone to break down unexpectedly, steam locomotives were so much faster than horses that soon they were pulling all the trains on the United States' infant railroad system. This consisted of numerous lines running from one nearby city to another, without connections to other lines.

When the first primitive railroads were built in the United States, beginning around 1830, the country's population still was concentrated close to the shore of the Atlantic Ocean. Groups of men in the major cities—Boston, New York, Philadelphia, Charleston, for example—tried their hands at railroad building. Nobody knew much about it. Every little railroad company was on its own, trying to solve unexpected problems. Americans realized that a wonderful new way to travel had been created that would carry them long distances toward the westward-pushing frontier. Communities in the wilderness that were isolated from each other by days of mud and dust and trudging, horse-drawn vehicles suddenly found themselves tied to the outer world. Emily Dickinson, the poet, speaking of the "grand railroad decision" made by her father and other businessmen of Amherst to bring the line to that New England village, said, "Nobody believes it. It seems like a fairy tale, a most miraculous event in the lives of all of us."

Marvelous as it seemed to those in their path, the railroads faced vexing difficulties of construction through forests and swamps, across rivers and through the Appalachian Mountains. Often tracks were laid hastily along the ground without proper roadbeds. Flimsy wooden bridges were thrown up, only to collapse when trains crossed them. Tracks were uneven, causing frequent derailments. Carelessly built boilers burst, with fatalities among crews and passengers. America was hungry for the benefits that railroads brought, and through the greed of some men and the inexperience of others paid a high price in lives to obtain them.

Some railroads experimented with putting down roadbeds of solid, smooth rock, then laying tracks of wood with metal strips on the hard bed. This was far too expensive and made for hard riding, too. The more general practice, which finally was adopted everywhere, was to lay wooden crossties on the dirt and string the rails along the crossties—fundamentally what railroads do today, except that they have added crushed stone ballast between the ties.

Many kinds of unexpected questions disturbed the men who ran the first railroads. Should they operate their trains on Sunday? "No!" said church leaders. That would be against the Bible. So, at first, no trains ran on Sunday, to the displeasure of those who weren't so religious and wanted to travel. This restriction began to break down. One short New England railroad stated on its timetables: "Persons purchasing tickets for Sunday trains will be required to sign a pledge that they will use the tickets for no other purpose than attending church."

How about running the trains at night? Nobody opposed the idea, but the difficulty was in how to light the track ahead of the locomotives. One railroad placed two flatcars at the front of a train, to be pushed by the locomotive. The first had a bed of sand, on which an urn-like structure of iron bars was constructed. Pine knots were dumped in this container and set ablaze, illuminating the track ahead with an eerie, flickering light. The second flatcar nearer the locomotive was for protection of the engineer from fire. One of the first locomotives built in this country, named *Best Friend*—all locomotives were given names at first—blew up in South Carolina in 1831. This frightened would-be passengers. So the railroad management placed a flatcar between the locomotive and passenger cars of each train and loaded it with bales of cotton as a buffer.

In Pennsylvania, a plague of grasshoppers chewed up fields of grain and settled on the railroad tracks, making them too slippery for the trains to use. Somebody said, "We'll put boxes of sand by the wheels of the locomotive and drop the sand on the tracks. That should make the wheels hold to the rails and turn." The idea worked, and sand boxes became standard equipment on locomotives from then on.

By trial and error of this kind, early trains began to look a little bit like the trains the world came to know later. On *Tom Thumb* and other early locomotives, the boiler stood upright. The engineer stood in the open, regardless of the weather, protected only by a railing on either side. After the boiler was laid flat, pointing toward the front of the locomotive instead of toward the sky, an ingenious fellow built a skimpy shed behind the boiler to cover the engineer. From that came the engineer's cab, where the engineer sat in overalls, long visored cap, and gloves, one hand on the throttle, his right elbow on the high windowsill, his eyes peering down the track, a kingly figure that small boys worshiped and

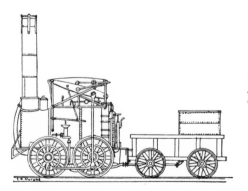

Boilers on the earliest trains stood upright, as on the Tom Thumb *and in this early sketch.*

The Rocket *was one of the first English locomotives. It averaged fifteen miles an hour on its first run on the Liverpool and Manchester Railway. Its boiler was six feet long.*

hoped to imitate some day. Asked what he wanted to be when he grew up, many a small boy had trouble deciding whether to be a fireman, who slid down a brass pole in the firehouse and dashed to fires behind the snorting pairs of fire horses, or a locomotive engineer. For a boy in the late 1800's it was a terrible decision to face; luckily, in most cases, the problem solved itself long before he was old enough to go to work in either job.

Every railroad had its own opinion about how far apart the rails should be. Nobody thought in those days that the federal government should decide a question like that; therefore, many different widths, or gauges, of track went into use. Often when two railroad lines crossed or ran close together, cars and engines couldn't be switched from one to the other because of a difference in track width. Railroads tried to solve the difficulty by laying two or even three parallel rails on one side of a track, each a calculated distance from the single rail on the other side, thus creating a line with two or three gauges. It was a costly, clumsy makeshift.

The first locomotives imported from England had wheels 4'8½"

29

apart, the gauge generally used in that country. A story that this was precisely the distance between the ruts of old Roman chariot roads in England is romantic but probably false. Thus pioneer American railroads that used locomotives from England used the English gauge. The dispute went on for more than thirty years, growing more bothersome as railroads were extended from one city to another and attempts were made to join them together. In the early 1860's, Abraham Lincoln decided that 4′8½″ would be the gauge used by the Union Pacific Railroad when it was built into the West with government financial help. This fairly well settled the matter. Today that is the standard gauge nationwide, except for a few narrow gauge tracks in the mountains.

Early locomotives burned wood, not coal. This required the stacking of small logs on the locomotive tender, which the fireman tossed into the engine's firebox to keep up steam. Since large areas of the Eastern, Southern, and Midwestern states were forested, fuel for the locomotives was easily at hand, waiting to be cut and stacked. Woodpiles of four-foot logs were built up along the track every twenty or twenty-five miles, at which the trains stopped while crewmen replenished the locomotive's supplies. Water for the engines was another essential. Until trackside water tanks were built at a later time, it was common to see bucket brigades of trainmen, sometimes helped by passengers, hauling water up from a stream to provide the engine with the liquid it needed to generate steam. This is the source of the expression "jerkwater railroad."

Burning wood in the locomotive boilers showered sparks out of the smokestacks, creating a menace. A wood-burning train chuffing through forests and prairies was like a traveling torch. Flying embers caused grass and forest fires, burned passengers, and occasionally were known to set the wooden coaches ablaze. Pictures of locomotives around the time of the Civil War showed them with bulky smokestacks shaped either like iron balloons or diamonds. This width made possible the insertion of a screen or baffle arrangement inside the stack to catch some of the sparks.

A writer describing passenger trains of the 1850's starting up from a station said, "Great balloon smokestacks would belch

30

The locomotive Pioneer *went into service on the Chicago and North Western Railway in 1848 and was retired in 1873 after hauling passenger and work trains. Note the ballooning smokestack. The locomotive has been repainted and put on public display.*

flame . . . the great yellow eyes of the huge whale-oil headlights pierced the night."

If all this sounds primitive, pity the plight of early-day passengers. Traveling by train at twenty miles an hour seemed marvelously swift, but it was rugged riding. The open coaches first used on the Baltimore and Ohio gave no protection from cold, wet weather. These were replaced by enclosed passenger cars that resembled long boxes on wheels with wooden steps at either end and small, high windows. Passengers sat on long wooden benches, swaying with the motion of the poorly cushioned cars. Ventilation was terrible. When the windows were open, sparks, cinders, and dust from the roadbed smeared the travelers. When the windows were closed, the stoves at either end of the coach kept the close-by areas warm while passengers in the middle of

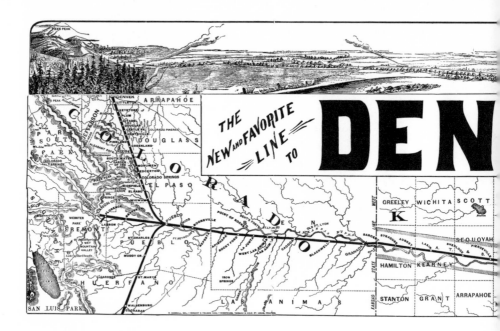

the car shivered. The stoves were fastened to the wall, so they would not spill out flames and ignite the coach in case of the all-too-frequent derailments. At night, tallow candles provided the only light and were a constant danger of fire. Coupling arrangements between cars were so poor that when a train started from a station the cars shook with a series of jerk-jerk-jerk motions until the locomotive picked up the slack.

Today, air brakes bring trains to a smooth halt. No such safe, convenient system existed until George Westinghouse invented one in 1869. Every coach was controlled by a hand brake in the form of a knobbed horizontal wheel on the outside platform. When the train slowed for a station, a brakeman on each coach turned the wheel, which clamped brakes against the coach wheels. No way existed for the conductor at the rear of the train to make contact with the engineer, up front, until an ingenious trainman thought of running a bell cord through all the coaches, near the ceiling. The conductor could send signals to the locomotive by prearranged pulls on this cord. Occasionally, an engineer would receive a long, continuous signal on the cord, his notice for an

32

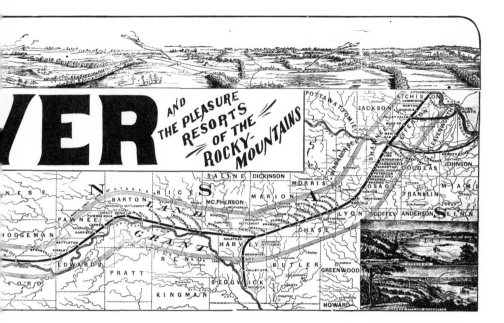

emergency stop.

"Why did you stop?" the conductor would ask.

"You signaled," the engineer replied.

"No, I didn't."

Whereupon a search of the train would be made, and almost invariably the crewmen would find an overcoat hanging from the bell cord, placed there by a backwoods passenger, riding a train for the first time, who thought it was a coatrack.

Primitive and rickety as these pioneer trains were, Americans developed an insatiable appetite for railroads and new lines were built as rapidly as work crews could do so. The country as far west as the Mississippi River and beyond to the Missouri River was being opened for settlement. Wherever a railroad reached, crowds of settlers traveled, intent on making new homes in the wilderness. In the ten years between *Tom Thumb*'s race with the horse in 1830 and 1840, almost five thousand miles of steam railroad lines were built in the United States, the largest portion of them in New York and Pennsylvania.

4

HORACE GREELEY TAKES A RIDE

Horace Greeley, the thundering New York editor who grew famous before the Civil War and proclaimed, "Go West, young man, go West!" followed his own advice to some extent in 1853. His purpose was not to settle but to give lectures to the inhabitants of the raw frontier towns of Indiana and Illinois on the evils of liquor. Greeley was a renowned temperance speaker, ready to suffer inconvenience and hardship in order to spread his message. Traveling by train on the recently established railroads of those sparsely developed states, discomfort is precisely what he found, in greater quantity than he had reckoned.

Greeley had spoken at Lafayette, in western Indiana. His next engagement was at La Porte, another community of a few hundred inhabitants some ninety miles to the north. The New Albany & Salem Railroad provided passenger service between the two towns, then on to Michigan City and Chicago, so Greeley's trip appeared to be relatively easy. Or so he thought, when he went to the station at Lafayette to board "the cars." The train itself was enough to shake him a little. Later, in a dispatch to his New York *Tribune*, he described it: "Five cars closely packed with hogs, five ditto with wheat, two ditto with lumber, three or four with livestock and notions returning from the fair, and two or three cattle cars containing passengers."

The locomotive, he said, was old and asthmatic, too weak to

haul such a load. The passengers quickly found that their coaches were much better suited for their original job of carrying cattle than for accommodating humans.

The train pulled out from Lafayette, along tracks laid up the middle of a street, at noon Sunday. Three hours later it had grunted and groaned its way as far as the country station of Brookston, fourteen miles north of Lafayette with, as Greeley put it, "a fair prospect of traversing our ninety odd miles by the dawn of Monday morning."

At Brookston, however, the locomotive needed wood and water. Since neither was available, the engineer uncoupled the locomotive and ran it five miles ahead for water. The next stack of wood was even farther along the track. Two hours later the re-plenished locomotive returned, was hooked onto the train, and the conductor hopefully called, "All aboard!" Away went the

This Illinois Central train was photographed at Kankakee, Illinois, in 1854 while opening passenger service between Chicago and Urbana, Illinois. It was typical of Midwestern trains of that period. Note diamond-shaped smokestack.

mixed train, for precisely half a mile. There the cock of the boiler blew off, draining off the water and steam so the engine was left powerless.

No telegraph lines existed along the New Albany & Salem. Telephones were still thirty years in the future. So the train was stranded in sparsely settled woody marshland, its whereabouts unknown to the rest of the world. The engineer of Greeley's train remembered, however, that another locomotive—a good one, he said—was parked at Culvertown, forty-three miles to the north. He proposed to take a handcar, a little railroad service vehicle propelled in those days by men pumping up and down alternately on cross handlebars like teeter-totters, up to Culvertown and bring back this locomotive.

Greeley and a few other passengers figured that anything was better than sitting indefinitely at Brookston, so they decided to go along. His claw-hammer coattails flapping, his beaver top hat slightly askew, the New York editor tossed his carpetbag onto the handcar and climbed aboard. Under a full moon but with no headlights, the seven men on the handcar divided into pairs on each handlebar and started pumping north. The task was, Greeley said, about like turning a heavy, two-handed grindstone. He wrote, "The car, equal in size to about a wheelbarrow and a half, just managed to hold us and give the propellors working room. To economize space, I sat a good part of the time facing backwards, with my feet dangling over the rear of the car, knocking here or there on a tie or a bridge timber, and often tickled through my boots by the coarse, rank weeds growing up at intervals between the ties and recently stiffened by hard October frosts."

The self-propelled passengers, invigorated by the night chill, pumped so strenuously that they made five miles in twenty-five minutes. Then their arms grew weary and their speed faltered. They stopped often for water and to recharge themselves from their supply of other liquid, in which Greeley could not join because of his temperance principles, so five hours passed before they reached Culvertown at midnight. Aside from the moon, their only illumination had been prairie fires they saw burning at four

THE SHEFFIELD VELOCIPEDE HAND-CAR !

CRERAR, ADAMS & CO.,
11 & 13 FIFTH AVE., AND 205 & 207 S. WATER ST., CHICAGO, ILLS.
AGENTS.

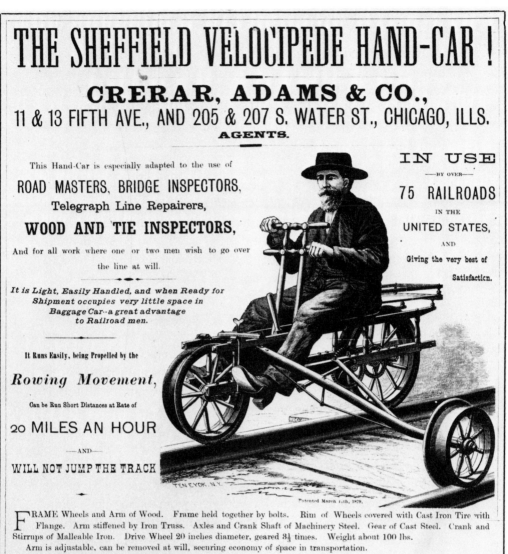

This Hand-Car is especially adapted to the use of

ROAD MASTERS, BRIDGE INSPECTORS,
Telegraph Line Repairers,

WOOD AND TIE INSPECTORS,

And for all work where one or two men wish to go over the line at will.

It is Light, Easily Handled, and when Ready for Shipment occupies very little space in Baggage Car--a great advantage to Railroad men.

It Runs Easily, being Propelled by the

Rowing Movement,

Can be Run Short Distances at Rate of

20 MILES AN HOUR

----AND----

WILL NOT JUMP THE TRACK

IN USE
----BY OVER----
75 RAILROADS
IN THE
UNITED STATES,
AND
Giving the very best of
Satisfaction.

Patented March 11th, 1879.

FRAME Wheels and Arm of Wood. Frame held together by bolts. Rim of Wheels covered with Cast Iron Tire with Flange. Arm stiffened by Iron Truss. Axles and Crank Shaft of Machinery Steel. Gear of Cast Steel. Crank and Stirrups of Malleable Iron. Drive Wheel 20 inches diameter, geared 3¼ times. Weight about 100 lbs.

Arm is adjustable, can be removed at will, securing economy of space in transportation.

Power is applied by hand lever in front of operator, and by stirrups for feet, which are connected to lower end of levers. The handle between the levers govern the brake.

The machine may be made to carry an extra person by leaving off rail back of operator, and placing an adjustable foot-rest below for the feet. Where they are used to any great extent for this purpose, a 17 inch driver is used instead of 20.

Machine can be run 8 to 10 miles an hour with perfect ease, and a speed of 12 to 18 miles can be attained with very little exertion. The inventor has many times made a run of thirty miles in less than two hours.

These machines are already largely in use on many of the American lines with *great success*, and the demand is *rapidly* increasing. Every machine warranted as represented.

The handcar Horace Greeley and six other men used in Indiana in 1853 was larger than the one pictured here.

places. Wild animals, scared by the handcar, had scurried across the track.

The rescue locomotive at Culvertown proved to be elusive. Somebody had driven it to Michigan City. By now the renowned Greeley was in a fit. He was cold, tired, and still a long way from La Porte, where he was scheduled to speak the next day. His angry words on the printed page moved Presidents of the United States, but his profusely spoken words could do nothing to conjure up a locomotive at midnight in the backwoods of Indiana. Nor could he even find a driver with a team of horses he could hire to drive him to La Porte. He still was thirty-five miles from his destination. Either in sympathy or to get rid of the irate New Yorker, the engineer of the ill-fated New Albany & Salem train who had led the handcar expedition to Culvertown agreed to lend the handcar to Greeley. They wakened two Culvertown residents who were willing to join the editor. At one in the morning the determined editor and the two local men started up the track toward La Porte on the handcar, grunting into the small community at 9:00 A.M. Monday. That afternoon Greeley treated the residents of La Porte to his renowned lecture on the evils of drinking hard liquor, spiced no doubt by a few added observations about the evils of the New Albany & Salem.

Not all pioneer railroad passengers had such strenuous misadventures as the editor did, but uncertainty and discomfort were commonplace. Timetables were more of a wishful-thinking gesture than a promise of on-time performance. Prim guardians of the nation's morals questioned whether a woman traveling alone was behaving in a respectable manner, no matter how carefully she averted her eyes from the men around her. Yet women needed to travel, too, on family visits. The problem was solved by putting a ladies car on each train, usually the last one in the line. Women traveling alone or in groups, or accompanied by a gentleman, took their places in these ladies cars. An unaccompanied man who dared to enter the ladies car was considered a cad. No smoking was permitted in these cars. If any daring young woman dreamed secretly of venturing forward into the uncouth, cigar-reeking world of the men's cars to smoke a cigarette, she quickly suppressed such a wild impulse. Her reputation would be ruined. Undoubtedly, half the elderly women in the ladies car would need to be revived by smelling salts at the enormity of such behavior.

Charles Dickens came to visit the United States in 1842 at the peak of his fame as a novelist and found that Americans at times weren't—well—quite what he thought they should be. They didn't act enough like his native Englishmen at times to suit him. He was impressed by the ladies cars on the trains, however, even if he did find them insufferably hot because of the coal stoves in the middle of the coaches. If he was hot, think how it must have been for the women with their billowing skirts, layers of petticoats, tightly laced corsets, and high collars!

"If a lady take a fancy to any male passenger's seat, the gentleman who accompanies her gives him notice of the fact, and he immediately vacates it with great politeness," Dickens reported to his English readers in amazement.

Riding a train through New England, he found little to see except mile after mile of woods and swamps.

"The train calls at stations in the woods where the wild impossibility of anybody having the smallest reason to get out, is only equalled by the apparently desperate hopelessness of there being anybody to get in," he wrote. "It rushes across the turnpike road, where there is no gate, no policeman, no signal: nothing but a rough wooden arch on which is printed, 'When the Bell Rings, Look Out for the Locomotive.' On it whirls headlong, dives through the woods again, emerges in the light, clatters over frail arches, rumbles upon the heavy ground, shoots beneath a wooden bridge which intercepts the light for a second like a wink, suddenly awakens all the slumbering echoes in the main street of a large town, and dashes on haphazard, pell-mell, neck-or-nothing, down the middle of the road. There—with mechanics working at their trades, and people leaning from their doors and boys flying kites and playing marbles, and men smoking and women talking, and children crawling and pigs burrowing, and unaccustomed horses plunging and rearing—there—on, on, on—tears the mad dragon of an engine with a train of cars; scattering in all direc-

Old print shows railroad tracks and trestles in Eastern United States. Charles Dickens described a train trip through such peaceful scenes in the 1840's.

tions a shower of burning sparks from its wood fire; screeching, hissing, yelling, panting; until at last the thirsty monster stops beneath a covered way to drink, the people cluster around, and you have time to breathe again."

Reading Dickens' almost breathless account of an early American train ride, we find it difficult to remember that in fact the train was traveling perhaps at twenty miles an hour. But speeds are comparative, and the picture he gives of the impact of train travel both on those aboard the cars and those on the ground watching is graphic.

By the time Lincoln became President, travel by train was the generally accepted method between cities, although reaching obscure places "by the cars" was difficult and at times impossible. An account of his trip from Washington to the Gettysburg, Pennsylvania, battlefield to deliver his immortal Gettysburg Address gives us an idea of what train travel was like during the Civil War.

Although the direct distance between the national capital and Gettysburg is about sixty miles, Lincoln found the round trip by train in a single day to be impossible. He traveled from Washington to Baltimore on a four-car train. The rear coach resembled a flat-topped wood box, with an open rear platform. A wooden wall partitioned off the back portion of the car, which President Lincoln used as a drawing room. As the train rolled along at twenty-five miles an hour, passengers from the rest of the train were allowed to visit him for a few minutes each.

The train arrived at the Camden Station in Baltimore on the Baltimore and Ohio tracks. The locomotive was disconnected and a team of horses hooked to the front car. The horses pulled the four cars through the city, along tracks down the center of Howard and Cathedral Streets, while a large crowd walked alongside, talking with passengers standing on the platforms and leaning from the windows.

Several times as the train moved at a horse's pace across the city, Lincoln stepped onto the rear platform and talked with the crowd. Mothers held their babies up to the gaunt, sallow-faced President and he kissed the infants in the standard political gesture of the period. The mothers beamed with delight, although the babies were less enthused about the scratchy Presidential bristles.

At the Western Maryland Railway station, the horses were replaced by a locomotive. Behind it a baggage car was hooked on, fitted with tables at which Lincoln and the other passengers were served a lunch that had been prepared and brought aboard.

A popular story persists that Lincoln wrote his brief, renowned Gettysburg Address on the back of an envelope during this tedious train ride. Most experts on Lincoln's life believe this is untrue, although he certainly gave the speech some thought as he rode.

41

Railroads gave free tickets to ministers in early days. This ticket was issued in 1863.

He may even have jotted down a note or two. The facts appear to be that he prepared a draft of the speech before leaving Washington, then polished the final text during his overnight stay at Gettysburg before driving by carriage to the dedication site at the new battlefield national cemetery.

As the short railroad lines between cities stretched out and linked up with each other, a traveler was able to undertake long trips; all the way from Philadelphia to St. Louis, for example. Usually this meant frequent changes of trains and long, dull waits in railroad stations to make connections. Each line issued a ticket just for its section, until someone conceived the idea of long perforated tickets, often measuring eighteen inches. A portion of the ticket was torn off by the conductor on each train, until by the time the passenger reached his destination he had only the stub of his once lengthy ticket left.

Practical as this new idea was, it confused many travelers at first. The story is told of a United States Senator from a newly organized Pacific Coast state who had never seen a train. He had come East by ship via the Isthmus of Panama, crossing the Isthmus by horse and continuing by ship to New Orleans. In the South he had boarded a train for Cincinnati, en route to take his senatorial seat in Washington. For the first time he saw a train conductor, who asked for the Senator's ticket. The conductor wore civilian clothes and looked like the passengers. Some lines dressed their conductors in top hats with a metal strip reading "Conductor" fastened with elastic. In the East, a few railroads that fancied themselves as aristocratic had their conductors wear frock coats and lilac kid gloves. These were the exceptions, however; most train conductors were like the one who approached the Senator, casual fellows who mixed their work with gossiping and yarn-spinning with the passengers.

The suspicious Senator refused to surrender his ticket, thinking the fellow wanted to steal it.

"I only want to look at it, sir," the conductor explained.

Dubiously, the Senator handed him the ticket. The conductor examined the coupons showing the routing, then tore off the coupon he needed.

That confirmed the Senator's suspicions. Angrily, he jumped from his seat, punched the conductor in the eye, and sent him sprawling into a seat across the aisle.

The assassination of President Lincoln in April, 1865, while he was attending a play at Ford's Theater in Washington a few days

Abraham Lincoln

after the end of the Civil War, tore at the hearts of the American people as they were emerging from four years of a devastating emotional turmoil. The funeral train that carried Lincoln's body on a long, roundabout journey from Washington, D.C., to his burial place in his home city of Springfield, Illinois, became a symbol of the national grief.

The journey from Washington to Springfield covered seventeen hundred miles, several hundred more than if the train had gone by a direct route, and required twelve days. An estimated million and a half persons filed silently past the coffin as it was placed on a bier in a public building in each of the major cities where the train stopped on its circuitous journey—Philadelphia, New York, Albany, Cleveland, Columbus, Indianapolis, Chicago. Some six million more Americans watched along the trackside as the black-draped train with the coffin in its rear car traveled slowly, usually through the night.

Much of the route westward was the same followed by Lincoln's train when he went from Illinois to Washington for his inauguration as President four years earlier; in fact, some of the same trainmen who had operated that earlier train served as crewmen on the farewell trip. In small cities crowds of ten thousand persons gathered at midnight and at 3:00 A.M. to watch the train pass. At tiny crossroads in the country, scores assembled by torchlight for the passing moment of silent tribute.

From Indianapolis the train moved at night to Lafayette, Indiana, and then north to Chicago along the same track on which Horace Greeley had been forced to pump himself out of the wilds by handcar a dozen years earlier.

At Chicago, the metropolis of the martyred President's home state, an outpouring of mourners, some 150,000, walked past the bier in the Cook Couny courthouse. While they were doing so, the funeral train was being made ready for the final leg of its trip, from Chicago to Springfield, along the tracks of the Chicago & Alton Railroad. Although the fact was obscured in the panoply of the funeral journey, a car that was to make railroad history was attached to the train for this overnight run. This was the newly completed *Pioneer*, the first successful sleeping car built by

44

Pullman cars had ornate interiors during the last half of the nineteenth century. The slanting panels above the seats are the bottoms of the upper berths. The Pioneer, the first car of this type, was added to Abraham Lincoln's funeral train for the use of Mrs. Lincoln.

George M. Pullman, the forerunner of the cars that became known universally as Pullmans and made possible comfortable night train travel.

Pullman had been experimenting with building sleeping accommodations on the standard wooden passenger cars of the day but with small success. The "berths" consisted of little more than flat wooden slabs, three tiers high; the mattresses on them were stacked at the end of the coach during the day.

In 1864 at Chicago, Pullman had started construction of the *Pioneer*, which embodied his new ideas, including a hinged upper berth that could be folded back to form the upper wall of the car during the day, its bedding contained inside. The *Pioneer* was a foot wider and two and a half feet higher than any railroad car then in service. It was attached to the Lincoln train to provide the most comfortable accommodations possible for Mrs. Lincoln and her family. Because of its size, station platforms along the Alton route had to be cut back and the sides and tops of bridges enlarged so it could pass through. The *Pioneer* passed its test successfully. Thus, by a wry twist of history, one of the country's great tragic moments became the proving ground for one of its most important transportation inventions.

5

BY TRAIN TO CALIFORNIA

From the raw frontier town of Omaha on the west bank of the Missouri River, a train of nine wooden cars pulled by two wood-burning locomotives puffed westward along the single railroad track that crossed the Nebraska prairie in the fall of 1866. Large American flags attached to the cowcatcher of the front locomotive whipped in the wind. The oil-burning headlight was adorned by a set of deer antlers, a decorative touch suggesting the Great West.

The two hundred prominent Americans and foreigners aboard the train were embarked on what was for most their first adventure into the West, into the land of hostile Indians and roaming herds of buffalo—not in a covered wagon but in the comfort and security of the most luxurious train yet to roll along the incompleted tracks of the transcontinental railroad to California. Among them were a future President of the United States, Rutherford B. Hayes, the late Abraham Lincoln's son Robert; generals from the recently ended Civil War in full dress uniforms; senators; governors; and foreign diplomats. Many were accompanied by their wives.

Officials of the Union Pacific Railroad, hosts for the train party, grandiosely named the expedition the Great Pacific Railway Excursion. The excursion wasn't going all the way to the Pacific Ocean, however, for the practical reason that a gap of many hun-

Union Pacific train carrying excursion party to railhead of transcontinental railroad in 1866 passes 100th meridian marker in Nebraska.

dreds of miles still existed in the railroad. Track-laying crews of the Central Pacific Railroad, building east from Sacramento, California, hadn't yet struggled through the massive barrier of the Sierra Nevadas. The Union Pacific, building west from Omaha, had laid track past the One Hundredth Meridian in central Nebraska and was stabbing across the Great Plains at the rate of two miles a day, or even more.

The Great Pacific Railway Excursion was headed as far west as it could go, to the actual railhead that kept moving forward constantly.

At nightfall the train stopped and the guests stayed in an encampment of tents on the Plains, sleeping on mattresses filled with hay under buffalo robes. They ate their supper of wild game around campfires. The night silence of the open spaces was shattered by a shrieking, screaming band of Pawnee Indians. They ran into the shadowy firelight like dervishes and performed a frenzied dance.

"Don't be alarmed," Union Pacific officials soothed their startled guests. "These are friendly Indians. They are helping us."

Even this explanation was hardly enough for men and women whose evenings normally were spent in the brightly lit parlors of city homes. At dawn the next day the party was awakened by a bone-tingling kind of alarm clock—Pawnee war whoops. Again the nervous Easterners were on edge, looking anxiously to their hosts for reassurance. The Union Pacific did everything it could to give its guests a thrill. One night it even ignited a prairie fire for them. The next day, the train stopped while the passengers went on a buffalo hunt, and another time so they could watch a mock battle between Pawnees and braves dressed as the greatly feared Sioux. Naturally the pseudo-Sioux lost. In between these excitements, the travelers dined on elaborate meals served aboard the train. The men made frequent trips to the "refreshment" car.

Finally the train reached the end of the track, far out on the Plains. The guests climbed down from the coaches to watch the show that the Union Pacific really had brought them all this way to see. A gang of specially trained Irish workmen laid eight hundred feet of track in thirty minutes. The visitors were amazed by the assembly-line techniques used by the gang—some men hauled rails from the pile that had been brought forward at dawn by the supply train, others heaved wooden ties into place, still others laid the rails and spiked them into position on the previously leveled grade. This grade could be seen stretching for miles ahead, awaiting the track. Full of awe at what they had seen, the eminent guests returned to their Eastern homes convinced that a wonderful thing was taking place in the building of the railroad that soon would tie together the Atlantic and Pacific Coasts of the

Passengers and trainmen shoot buffalo from a galloping herd on the Great Plains in the 1870's.

The railroad across the Great Plains was built by muscle, sweat, and iron. Many Irishmen worked in Union Pacific track crews.

United States with an unbroken iron band.

Construction of the transcontinental railroad was a wonderful thing, indeed, and far more difficult than the pampered guests on the Great Pacific Railway Excursion realized. More than six years passed from the time the first rail was laid by the Central Pacific at Sacramento until the track across the country was complete and trains at last could run from coast to coast.

For the Central Pacific, building eastward, the lofty snow-crowned peaks of the Sierras were the greatest challenge. Charles Crocker, in charge of construction, brought thousands of Chinese coolies into the mountains to build the grade for the track. Most of them spoke no English. The setting was about as remote from their Oriental homeland as it could possibly be, but they were tireless workers. The most formidable barrier blocking the route was a towering rock formation known as Cape Horn. Using blasting powder and hanging from the rocks over the deep canyon by ropes, the swarms of Chinese hacked out a ledge yard by yard along the side of the formation, until the track could be laid around it. At other points, tunnels were dug with hand tools and blasting powder. In winter, huge snows at the highest levels blocked the track. Crocker overcame this obstacle by construct-

Unloading ties and rails during the construction of the transcontinental railroad

A Union Pacific work train at the railhead unloads materials to be carried forward by freight wagons to track crews building the transcontinental railroad.

Heavy drifts piled up against the snow sheds that protected the track of the Central Pacific Railroad in the high mountain passes.

ing miles of snow sheds over the right-of-way. These had sloping roofs from which the snow slid into the valley below. The sheds, forming long wooden tunnels, made it possible for the trains to operate all winter.

After years of discouraging labor, the Central Pacific track finally crossed over the Donner Summit, close to the spot where the Donner emigrant party became snowbound a quarter century earlier and suffered one of the grimmest tragedies in the opening of the West. The track advanced down the eastern slope of the Sierras and across the parched desert of Nevada toward Utah. The rails, the locomotives, and most of the equipment for the Central Pacific had been hauled to California from the East Coast by sailing ship around Cape Horn. Now the railroad was moving eastward back toward the sources from which the materials had come.

Although they were engaged in a joint venture of building the cross-country railroad, the Central Pacific and the Union Pacific were rivals, almost enemies. For every mile of track completed, the federal government paid each company generous subsidies. Track laid in the mountains was worth more per mile than that laid across the flat Plains because the job was so much more difficult. It was a race all the way, each railroad trying to get the bigger share of government money and using tricky financial schemes to do it.

The Union Pacific got a later start than the Central Pacific by about two years. It, too, had to haul its track and locomotives from the East, mostly by steamboat up the Missouri River to

Interior of wooden snow shed built to protect the transcontinental track from heavy snowfalls and avalanches in the Sierra Nevadas.

Omaha. The danger of Indian attacks was constant. At times bands of Sioux and Cheyenne raided the construction parties, which always worked with guns at hand. But when its crews of Irish immigrants got rolling, the Union Pacific laid two miles of track a day, even more on rare days, across the table-top plains of Nebraska, over the crest of the Continental Divide and the lonely highlands of Wyoming, and down through a pass in the Wasatch Mountains of Utah into the Great Salt Lake Valley. Rough, brawling towns were born at the railhead overnight. Most of them died as the tracks advanced past them, but a few survived in diminished form and later became such important cities as North Platte, Nebraska, and Cheyenne and Laramie, Wyoming.

At last the track from the west and the track from the east met in the sagebrush desert at Promontory Point, Utah, north of the Great Salt Lake. On May 10, 1869, locomotives of the Central Pacific and the Union Pacific drew together until they were almost nose to nose. Leland Stanford, representing the Central Pacific, drove a golden spike into a crosstie of California laurel, fastening down the final rail in the 1700-mile line. A telegraph message sent by dot-dash from the scene set off jubilant celebrations from one coast to another. After years of waiting, travelers could cross the entire width of the United States by train. Gone were the days of the covered wagon and the stagecoach!

Today the line no longer goes past Promontory Point but further south. At the Golden Spike National Historical Site at Promontory, two old-style locomotives stand cowcatcher to cowcatcher on an unused section of track, a reminder to visitors of the historic linkup more than a century ago. Reenactment of the golden spike ceremony in summer is an attraction for tourists.

No sooner was the line complete than passenger trains began making cross-country trips daily. The station at Omaha bustled with sight-seeing travelers and with emigrants who were moving to new homes and starting new lives. Suddenly it had become much easier to follow Horace Greeley's advice about going West, young man, and growing up with the country.

The daily transcontinental train was named the Pacific Express westbound and the Atlantic Express eastbound from California.

A poster announces opening of the transcontinental railroad in 1869. Passengers from the East could travel to San Francisco by rail for the first time.

An early-day office of the Atlantic & Pacific Railroad on the West Coast. Notice the hats and gold watch chains worn by the men.

A motley group of travelers and Indians crowded the Union Pacific Railroad depot at Omaha in 1868.

Its locomotives had polished brass trimmings. The metal boxes encasing their oil headlights were decorated with elaborate red, green, and gold painted scrolls. The wheels of the locomotives were bright colors. On the panels beneath the engineer's window in ornate letters were the names of the locomotives—names like *C.P. Huntington* and *Leland Stanford*, for two of the Central Pacific's builders, and less personal ones like *Hercules, Growler, Diana,* and *Magpie.* The locomotives may have been slow, but they had the plumage of iron birds.

Although the track ran unbroken from Omaha to California, for years control of it was divided by the two companies. Passengers from the East had to change from a Union Pacific train to a Central Pacific train at Ogden, Utah, the nearest city to the place where the railroads had linked up at Promontory Point.

Train travel was much faster than the old covered wagons, but how comfortable was it? By our standards the trains were primitive and slow. Judging from accounts written by travelers on the transcontinental railroad in its early years, much depended upon where you rode, in a Pullman car with porters to attend you or in one of the crowded, smelly emigrant coaches.

Riding on the Pacific Railroad was much like going on a long sea voyage; for days the passengers were almost cut off from the rest of the world. Only a few small communities and an occasional cluster of wooden shacks along the track broke the endless miles of plains and desert. Once in a while the sight of antelope or a herd of buffalo broke the monotony.

A prominent writer, Charles Nordhoff, traveled from Chicago to California on the railroad in 1872 and wrote such a glowing account of the trip for *Harper's Magazine* that he sounded like a propagandist for the railroads. He traveled first class, a fact that unquestionably colored his outlook. From Chicago to Omaha, he reported, the train carried a dining car—"a great curiosity in its way." Dining cars still were a rare luxury on American trains. For one dollar the traveler could have a sumptuous dinner, choosing from a menu that included buffalo, elk, antelope, and grouse. A recently constructed bridge across the Missouri River allowed the train from Chicago to steam right into Omaha, where passengers

Ogden remained a transfer point for years. The boy in the photo is Stephen Vincent Benét, photographed in 1906. Note the Pullman car in the background.

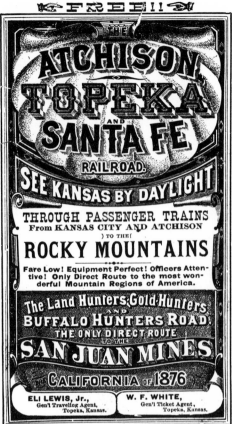

Timetable of the Centennial Year. The Atchison, Topeka and Santa Fe referred to itself as "The Land Hunters, Gold-Hunters and Buffalo Hunters Road."

Engineers sometimes used jets of live steam to drive buffalo from the track so the train could proceed. This enlivened the trip for the often bored passengers.

changed to the Union Pacific train.

No dining car was carried west of Omaha, but the train did have "hotel cars." The hotel car, which soon vanished from the railroads because it was impractical economically, was a luxurious self-contained coach whose small number of passengers slept in Pullman berths, lounged, and dined on food prepared right in the car. Those who traveled in Pullman sleeping cars, or more frugally and uncomfortably sat up all night in the coaches, ate their meals in restaurants alongside the track. The train made meal stops three times a day.

Nordhoff traveled by Pullman sleeping car. Without this accommodation, he admitted, the trip would have been extremely uncomfortable, but with it he found the long journey a joyous pleasure jaunt.

One of the nicest things about the cross-country trip, he said, was its length. The passenger could settle down for days of traveling and needn't worry about having to hustle off the train in a few hours, as travelers between Eastern cities did.

"You will never know how great a difference it makes to your comfort whether your train goes at the rate of forty (which Eastern trains did) or at twenty-two miles an hour," Nordhoff declared. "This last is the pace of the iron horse between Omaha and San Francisco; and it is to the fierce and rapid rush of an Eastern lightning express what a gentle and easy amble is to a rough and jolting trot."

At twenty-two miles an hour, the Western traveler had abundant time to see the countryside, a fact that Nordhoff thought was splendid. He didn't mention that for hundreds of miles from Omaha the scenery had an eye-dulling monotony. Slow as that speed seems, the train still traveled more miles in an hour than a covered wagon did in a day.

"At thirty-five or forty miles an hour the country you pass through is a blur," Nordhoff wrote. "One hardly sees between the telegraph poles; pleasure and ease are out of the question; reading tires your eyes, writing is impossible, conversation impractical except at the auctioneer pitch, and the motion is wearing and tiresome." It was enough to sicken a sensitive stomach. But at

59

twenty-two miles an hour—ah, a man could really see the country and digest his meals in comfort! "Your housekeeping is done by alert and experienced servants . . . you may pursue all the sedentary avocations and amusements of a parlor at home."

Traveling in such style, Nordhoff enthused about everything he saw. The trip came to a spectacular climax on the journey's last day in California. Let him tell it:

". . . the grand and exciting rush down the Sierra from Summit to Colfax, winding around Cape Horn and half a hundred more precipitous cliffs, down which you look out of an open observation car, as you sweep down from a height of 7,000 feet to a level of 2,500 in a ride of two hours and a half. A grander or more exhilarating ride than from Summit to Colfax on the Central Pacific Railroad you cannot find in the world. The scenery is various, novel and magnificent. You sit in an open car at the end of

Passengers on the transcontinental train sat in an outdoor observation car to watch the descent through the Sierra Nevadas to California.

An emigrant train and locomotive, photographed about 1869 during a pause on the long, slow trip to the West.

the train, and the roar of the wind, the rush and vehement impulse of the train, the whirl around curves past the edge of deep chasms, among forests of magnificent trees, fill you with excitement, wonder, and delight."

After five days of riding the train from Chicago at slow speed, no doubt most passengers found part of the thrill of this final morning in the fact that they were about to get off the cars, at last. Few of them shared Nordhoff's patience.

A few years later Robert Louis Stevenson made the same transcontinental train trip. Because he had so little money, he rode in an emigrant car. He had not yet written *Treasure Island* and other books that were to make him famous but was only a frail, impoverished young Scotsman going to California for his health and to be married. Nevertheless, enough of a literary air surrounded him that his rough-and-ready companions on the train nicknamed him "Shakespeare." He refused to tell them his real name, just to spite them because they were so curious about it. The long train ride about which Nordhoff enthused so much was a miserable and boring experience for him.

Stevenson described the typical Union Pacific coach as a "long, narrow wooden box, like a flat-roofed Noah's Ark," lighted by lamps that often went out and shed but a dying glimmer even when they burned. A stove stood at one end of the car and a toilet at the other end. Seats were so narrow that two men barely could sit side by side. The coach had open-air platforms with iron guard railings at each end.

The emigrants on the train were divided into three cars—women in one, men in another, and Chinese men in a third. On the all-male emigrant coach to which Stevenson was assigned, sleeping was done on a makeshift basis. A trainman sold passengers a board and three square cushions stuffed with straw. At night, the reversible backs of the seats were turned so that pairs of seats faced each other. Two passengers laid their boards side by side from one seat to the other, forming a shelf-like wooden

Robert Louis Stevenson as a young man, about the time he traveled to California aboard an emigrant train

platform on which they placed their cushions. This created a bed for the two passengers to lie side by side and try to sleep. The plank bed was hardly long enough for medium-sized men. A tall man was out of luck. Those who could not afford boards and cushions slept on the floor.

On the first night out from Omaha, Stevenson recounted later in *Across the Plains*, a fellow passenger played songs on his cornet and others joined in raucous singing. As darkness fell, the men laid their pairs of planks across the seats and prepared to sleep in their clothes, if they could. The train stopped at a little station on the Plains, and an unexpected thing happened.

"The cars were instantly thronged with the natives, wives and fathers, young men and maidens, some of them in little more than nightgear, some with stable lanterns, and all offering beds for sale. Their charge began with twenty-five cents a cushion, but fell, before the train went on again, to fifteen, with the bed-board gratis, or less than one fifth of what I had paid for mine."

A newsboy walked through the coach selling food, soap, towels, and washpans. Early the next morning, after a restless night, Stevenson teamed up with two other men nicknamed "Dubuque" and "Pennsylvania." Shakespeare bought a tin washing dish, Dubuque a towel, and Pennsylvania a brick of soap. They took turns in giving themselves a pre-breakfast washing.

Stevenson described this operation: "Each filled the tin dish at the water filter opposite the stove, and retired with the whole stock in trade to the platform of the car. There he knelt down, supporting himself by a shoulder against the woodwork or one elbow crooked about the railing, and made a shift to wash his face and neck and hands; a cold, inefficient, and if the train is moving rapidly, a somewhat dangerous toilet."

He and his partners teamed up on food, too, each buying something and then combining their resources. Similar trios did the same thing throughout the emigrant cars.

"Before the sun was up the stove would be brightly burning," he recalled. "At the first station the natives would come on board with milk and eggs and coffee cakes; and soon from end to end the car would be filled with little parties breakfasting upon the

Some passengers did their own cooking on the long Western train trips.
A drawing titled "The Modern Ship of the Plains" in Harper's Weekly,
1886.

bedboards. It was the pleasantest hour of the day."

The night the train left Laramie, Wyoming, Stevenson became
ill. We are fortunate that this master of the English language
with his wonderful flair for description has left us an account of
that miserable night. It gives an unforgettable picture of what
emigrants had to endure aboard these pioneer trains.

"The lamps did not go out; each made a faint shining in its own
neighborhood, and the shadows were confounded together in the
long, hollow box of the car. The sleepers lay in uneasy attitudes;
here two chums alongside, flat upon their backs like dead folk;
there a man sprawling on the floor, with his face upon his arm;
there another half-seated with his head and shoulders on the
bench. The most passive were continually and roughly shaken by
the movement of the train; others stirred, turned, or stretched out
their arms like children; it was surprising how many groaned or
murmured in their sleep; and as I passed to and fro, stepping
across the prostrate, and caught now a snore, now a gasp, now a

half-formed word, it gave me a measure of the worthlessness of rest in that unresting vehicle. Although it was chill, I was obliged to open my window, for the degradation of the air soon became intolerable. . . ."

Wealthy passengers riding in the hotel cars and Pullman sleepers watched the emigrants traveling on low-priced tickets with a shudder, wondering how they could bear to ride in such discomfort. The train conductors looked down sneeringly at the emigrants, too, often refusing to answer their questions or even to tell them when the train would make its next stop. Yet, unpleasant as the trip was for them, emigrants bore the hardships with relatively little grumbling because it was their cheap passage to a new life in the vastness of the West.

Within a few years another transcontinental route was opened by the Santa Fe Railroad across the Southwest to Los Angeles,

Artist's sketches show interior of a Pullman palace car on the Pacific Railroad, day and night.

and the Southern Pacific Railroad, which developed from the Central Pacific, built a cross-country line east from Los Angeles close to the American-Mexican border. Competition for passengers to the Pacific Coast was so intense that the railroads fought a price-cutting war. When the first transcontinental trains began, the first class fare from Chicago to San Francisco was $130. A dollar in those days bought much more than one does today.

Eager to attract passengers, Southern Pacific reduced the fare to $100. Santa Fe gave an even greater bargain. Down, down, down went the fares. Santa Fe offered to carry a passenger from the Missouri River to California for a mere $8.00. Southern Pacific undercut that to $6.00. For a few hours on March 6, 1887, both lines actually offered the trip for only $1.00. No wonder emigrants and sightseers traveled west by the scores of thousands.

As these travelers rode across the country, they constantly asked the question, "What time is it?" They asked not only from boredom, wondering how much of their trip was left, but from confusion. No organized system of time zones existed. Every city from the Atlantic to the Pacific was on its own, basing its local time on sun time, noon being the moment when the sun crossed the meridian. Since this varied by one minute for every thirteen miles east to west, cities only a relatively few miles apart operated on different times.

Every railroad had its own time standard, often based on the time used in a major city on its route. Things were so confused that in Pittsburgh, for example, the railroad station had six clocks, each showing a different time for the railroads using the terminal. You can imagine the mixups this caused among passengers hurrying to catch trains.

Railroads had at least sixty-eight different time standards, instead of the four in effect across the country today. A traveler going from Maine to California had to change his watch about twenty times in order to be synchronized with the areas through which the train was passing.

Even within cities, time was in a muddle. Watchmakers had different interpretations of the moment when the sun crossed the meridian. Residents set their watches to varying times, depending

Weary passengers settling down for the night on a long-distance train constantly asked each other, "What time is it?" From Frank Leslie's Illustrated Newspaper, 1878.

upon which watchmaker they trusted. Some railroads named a specific watchmaker in a city as the official keeper of the time and instructed their conductors and engineers to set their watches by the large clock in that merchant's window. This led to the creation of the time ball, a long-forgotten feature of city life. It was a ball three or four feet in diameter, mounted on a high pole. Precisely at noon, the designated city timekeeper released the ball, which fell to the bottom of the pole. That moment was officially noon in the city, and thousands of residents checked their watches against the fall of the ball. This method got all the timepieces in a city coordinated, but it did nothing to untangle the confusion between cities.

Since the railroads and their passengers were the worst sufferers, the railroads took it upon themselves to solve the problem. They called a General Time Convention in Chicago in October,

67

1883, which adopted the Standard Time system. They divided the country into four zones—Eastern, Central, Mountain, and Pacific. All cities within each zone set their clocks identically, even though this put noon in many cities several minutes off true sun time.

The railroads agreed that they would switch over their clocks to the Standard Time system precisely at noon Sunday, November 18, 1883. That Sunday was a day with two noons, the old local sun time noon and the new Standard Time noon. Clocks had to be changed as much as forty-four minutes to bring the cities into line. While most Americans, especially railroad travelers, welcomed the new system, others complained or were confused. Some believed that minutes were being taken out of their lives.

"Sun time is the natural way," the protestors said. "You are destroying God's will!"

The mayor of Bangor, Maine, felt so strongly about this that he threatened to have the police stop churches from ringing their bells on the new time. Actually, no law existed to make cities adopt the Standard Time system, which was only an agreement among the railroads, but the advantages of the method were so evident that cities everywhere quickly fell into line. Not until another twenty-five years had passed, however, did Congress get around to passing the Standard Time Act that made the four time zones a matter of law. That was in 1918.

When Daylight Saving Time became popular, the railroads had a new problem. Some states and cities went to Daylight Saving Time in summer, others didn't. So the railroads, except the commuter lines near the big cities, continued to run their trains by Standard Time the seasons around for years, and passengers had to be sure to translate the difference when they caught a train. When someone refers to "railroad time," he means Standard Time.

6

"SPECIAL VARNISH"

If a wealthy man wishes to travel in exclusive style today, he buys an executive jet airplane and flies around the country at his whim without concerning himself with airline schedules and reservations. At the turn of the twentieth century, rich men and women showed off their wealth in a similar way by having private railroad cars. These elaborately fitted coaches were attached to the rear of scheduled passenger trains. If a plutocrat, as such men were called then, desired to show off in even more flamboyant style, he rented an entire special train and attached his private car to it, turning over the rest of the train to his guests. In the railroad slang of the day, passenger trains were "varnish" because of the shiny finish applied to the wooden cars. Private cars and trains were "special varnish."

Possessors of private cars tried to outdo each other in their furnishings and style of living, usually letting news of their extravagances leak out to the newspapers and magazines. These published feature stories about the luxuries, which were read by passengers in the hard, dusty daycoach seats with either envy or disgust.

Some private cars were adorned with crystal chandeliers, marble bathtubs, wood-burning fireplaces, and wine cellars. French chefs were employed to provide gourmet meals. A Hungarian countess visiting this country hired a private Pullman, on

This artist gave readers of the Illustrated London News *an idealized view of Sunday on a Union Pacific train in 1875. Elegant as these trains were, the private cars of the day surpassed them.*

which she had her liveried footmen serve meals on her own set of gold plates. The millionaire August Belmont adorned his private car with hatracks of solid silver shaped like the horns of a stag. Pullman berths were not good enough for him and his guests; his car was equipped with brass beds, which were regarded as a symbol of affluence.

Not all of these furnishings on private cars were practical, splendid as they sounded. When the singing star Fritzi Scheff toured the country in Victor Herbert's operetta *Kiss Me Again*, she did so in a special car equipped with a full length bathtub. Alas, the glamorous Miss Scheff discovered that if she took a bath when the train was moving, the motion splashed water over the side of the tub and drenched the floor. So she scheduled her baths when the train was making a stop of twenty minutes or longer.

Perhaps the ultimate in showing off on wheels came when George Gould, son of the Erie Railroad tycoon Jay Gould, assembled a private train of five Pullman palace cars, invited a large number of guests to travel with him, and insisted that they appear for dinner in full evening dress. They were attended at

Guests sit down to elaborate dinner aboard private railroad car.

dinner by servants wearing black satin knee breeches and crimson tailcoats with gold trim.

Leland Stanford, president of the Central Pacific and governor of California, received an appropriate gift from his wife one year, his own private car. It even bore his own name, the *Stanford*. Some years after his death, the car passed into the possession of the Southern Pacific's general manager, Joseph Dyer. On one trip through the southwestern desert, Dyer had his son Joe with him. The Fourth of July was approaching and Joe had acquired a supply of firecrackers. When the car was at Yuma, Arizona, far out on the hottest part of the desert with the temperature well above 100 degrees Fahrenheit in the days before air conditioning, Joe couldn't resist experimenting with his fireworks. This was a tragic miscalculation. *Flash, bang, boom* went Joe's fireworks. *Whoosh!* A burst of flame ignited the wooden *Stanford*. The famous car burned down to its trucks, bringing an inglorious end to the first private car known in the Far West.

The most publicized of the early-day special private trains was the Lightning Express from New York to San Francisco in 1876, the Centennial Year. The trip involved a theatrical company and was carried out with a dramatic flair and much publicity. Henry C. Jarrett, a theater proprietor in New York, conceived the idea as a way to publicize the opening of Shakespeare's *Henry V* in San Francisco.

At that time, only seven years after the transcontinental railroad opened, the train trips from the East Coast to the West Coast required seven days and nights. Jarrett's plan was to move Lawrence Barrett and his *Henry V* company from New York to San Francisco in four days. The play was to close its Broadway run on Wednesday night and open its San Francisco booking the following Monday night. Undoubtedly the opening could have been delayed a day or two, but Jarrett wanted the tight schedule so he could promote the train race against time in the theatrical tradition that "the play must go on."

After the last curtain in the Booth Theater of New York on Wednesday night, the Shakespearian actors gathered for a late supper at the Astor Hotel on Broadway. Each was given a ticket

72

printed on silver, contained in a presentation box. From the Astor the company rode in horse cabs on the ferry to Jersey City, where the special train awaited them. As part of the publicity buildup, fifteen thousand copies of the New York *Herald* were loaded in the baggage car, to be sold on the streets of San Francisco. A reporter for the *Herald* was aboard, too; along the way, he wrote dispatches for his newspaper and the Associated Press, which he dropped off at stations to be telegraphed to New York. The train was a short one, consisting of the baggage car, a Pullman hotel car, and a Pullman sleeper.

Obviously, the train never would reach San Francisco in time for a Monday opening if it followed the railroad custom of that period of traveling at forty miles an hour on Eastern tracks and at a sedate twenty-two miles an hour on the long run west from Omaha. The word was given, "Go as fast as you can."

And fast it went. It rattled and shook at speeds rarely heard of in those early days of railroading. At one point the train's speed reached a spectacular sixty-two miles an hour. "More than a mile a minute!" the passengers exclaimed when informed of their swift pace.

Exciting as the trip sounded, the passengers found it extremely uncomfortable. The rails of that period were thin, light iron and the track ballast was poor. When the short train built up such speeds, it shook terribly, so badly that the men aboard didn't dare shave with their straight, open-blade "cut-throat" razors. As a result, they had a four-day growth of beard when they reached the Golden Gate. Cooking and serving hot food in the swaying cars was impossible. The porters had difficulty putting sheets on the Pullman berths because they had to hang on with both hands. Few of the passengers got much sleep.

Making things worse, the air line broke, knocking out the train's air brakes, so that when the train was to be slowed down or stopped, members of the crew had to turn the hand brake wheels by applying muscle to them. This created a perilous situation when the train rolled down the precipitous grades on the western slope of the Sierra Nevadas, still trying to make the fastest time it could. At one point the baggage car developed a smoking "hot

73

Old print shows train crossing the Rockies.

box" on one wheel. A Central Pacific crewman stood on the car's outside platform, leaned over the side of the train with one hand clinging to the guard rail, and with the other hand opened the journal box, the metal housing near the end of the axle covering the bearings. He stuffed fresh waste and lubricant around the axle while the train sped on. Anything to avoid stopping. Minutes were too precious.

As the train neared Reno, Nevada, the biggest town in hundreds of miles of desert, Jarrett announced that true to its name, it would rush through the little city "like a streak of lightning." He wanted to give both the passengers and the townspeople a thrill and, naturally, give the *Herald* reporter something to write home about. So he put a load of red fire, a material that flared brightly when ignited, on the tender behind the locomotive. Roman candles were distributed to the passengers. When the train reached the outskirts of Reno, the red fire was ignited into a sheet of flame. The passengers shot their Roman candles out of the open windows of their cars, causing hundreds of colored balls of fire to light up the night. Somebody in town fired a cannon in a return salute.

This was the kind of flamboyance that the citizens of San Francisco loved. They were out in force to welcome the Lightning Express when it pulled in, having made the cross-country trip in a record 83 hours and 59 minutes. A cannon on the roof of the Palace Hotel fired a thirteen-gun salute. The copies of the New York *Herald* were gobbled up by curious readers along Market Street, who were impressed to be reading a New York newspaper only four days after its publication. As for the bone-weary actors, they ate an elaborate breakfast in a restaurant whose floor was solid and whose tables didn't shake. Then they shaved off their scruffy beards, went to bed, and slept almost until curtain time. That Monday night *Henry V* opened on schedule.

While this was the most spectacular of all theatrical "special varnish," other celebrated performers in later years enjoyed the luxuries of private trains as they toured the country. One of these was Lillie Langtry, known as the "Jersey Lily" in the 1880's. Her private car *Lalee* (meaning "Flirt") attached to the rear of her special train was so elaborately equipped that it reminded one visitor of the barge on which Cleopatra traveled along the Nile River in ancient Egypt.

Miss Langtry's railroad car had solid silver bathroom fixtures, lace-trimmed silk curtains, overstuffed furniture, even a piano. Her maid's room contained a sewing machine for repairing her

Under the wheels

array of dresses. To give her theatrical caravan a touch of high society, the Jersey Lily had a butler in cutaway coat and top hat to direct operations and welcome guests. Naturally all this was made known to newspaper reporters, who recorded it for their readers and helped to build up Miss Langtry's glamorous image to the point that crusty Judge Roy Bean, who called himself "the law west of the Pecos," named his frontier town in Texas "Langtry" and gave the actress a raucous Western welcome when her train halted there during one of her tours.

Another famous actress who traveled the country in a special train was Sarah Bernhardt, the French dramatic star who billed herself as "the divine Sarah." She performed only in French, and often while seated on a sofa during the entire show because of a bad leg. Although most of her audiences in the smaller cities couldn't understand what she was saying, they flocked to her shows to see her emotional, gesturing performances and marvel at her marvelously controlled voice. Miss Bernhardt drew such crowds on her farewell tour of the United States that she made a second farewell tour, a third one, and finally a fourth.

She toured in a seven-car private train which one reporter described as almost a duplicate of the Twentieth Century Limited. Along with the stage scenery, it had accomodations for her party of thirty, with her private car at the end. While Miss Bernhardt was concerned about getting the local citizens' money at the box office in each city, she cared little about the citizens themselves and their towns. The train pulled onto a siding in a new city each morning. Often the actress didn't leave the train until evening, to go to the theater in a horse-drawn carriage. She kept the curtains of her private car drawn, so the curious onlookers could not see in. One night at Mobile, Alabama, a group of her admirers gathered outside the private car, calling for her to come out and greet them. The Divine Sarah was so angry at the audacity of the request that she opened the window of her bedroom and dumped a jug of water on her admirers' heads.

Death Valley Scotty wasn't an actor by trade, but he was "on stage" all the time, playing the role of a desert prospector who had struck it rich. He bragged about his secret gold mine some-

A replica of Death Valley Scotty's Coyote Special that made a record run from Los Angeles to Chicago. Engine #1010 was one of the locomotives used on the actual trip.

where in the hot sands and raw barren mountains of Death Valley in a remote corner of California. He built a million dollar Spanish castle at Grapevine Canyon in Death Valley and furnished it in ornate style with wagonloads of rich trappings hauled in by wagon a long distance over a narrow dirt road. Once in a while Scotty emerged from his desert hideout to visit Los Angeles, where he cut a boisterous swath in a ten-gallon hat and flannel shirt. He lit cigars with five-dollar bills, flashed a wad of hundred-dollar bills in the hotel, and tossed coins on the sidewalk, laughing uproariously as boys in the crowd that followed him scrambled to grab them.

One day in 1905 Scotty walked into the office of the Santa Fe Railroad general passenger agent in Los Angeles, tossed his hat into a corner, and announced, "I want to take a train on your road to Chicago. I want you to put me in there in forty-six hours. Kin you do it?"

"That is eleven hours and fifty-six minutes faster than the run has ever been made," the Santa Fe man replied.

Scotty pulled out a roll of thousand-dollar bills and started to lay them down, one by one. "I'm willing to pay any old figure. Kin you do it or can't you?" The Santa Fe man said his railroad could.

A few days later Scotty's special train, soon to be known nationwide as the Coyote Special, awaited him at the Los Angeles station. It consisted of three cars: a baggage car, diner, and sleeping car. Thousands of curious onlookers jammed around the train to cheer Scotty on his way. An automobile sped up to the station, the weather-beaten prospector jumped out, pushed his way through the crowd, climbed aboard the locomotive, shook hands with the engineer and fireman, then made a short speech from the tender.

"*Whoop-ti-do!*" he shouted. "Let's go."

Moments after Scotty had disappeared into the cars, the conductor raised his hand and called, "All aboard!" The big locomotive gathered momentum in a hurry and shortly disappeared down the track with its light load. It was a wild ride, wilder probably than Scotty ever had endured on a half-tamed horse. At one point the train hit a speed of 106 miles an hour. Scotty's party found it difficult to stand up inside the swaying cars. Mostly they remained seated and hung on. Scotty rode part of the time in the locomotive cab and shoveled coal into the fiery boiler. He handed out twenty-dollar gold pieces to each fresh crew whenever the train stopped for a change of locomotives. A reporter on the train dropped off news bulletins at each servicing stop, while publicity-wise Scotty shot off telegrams, including one from Dodge City, Kansas, to President Theodore Roosevelt announcing, "An American cowboy is coming east on a special train faster than any cowpuncher ever rode before." The message to Teddy Roosevelt was appropriate; everybody on Scotty's rocking, swaying train knew what it meant to be a Rough Rider.

Newspaper stories about the record-breaking attempt brought crowds to stations along the Santa Fe route to watch the Coyote Special speed through. The Santa Fe gave it a green signal all along the 2265-mile route.

After a tooth-shaking dash across the final stretch of Illinois prairie, the train rushed into the Polk Street station at Chicago almost at full speed, jamming on its brakes at the last moment. Scotty stepped from the Pullman, waving his big Stetson at the cheering welcomers. The train had made the trip in 44 hours and 54 minutes, more than an hour faster than the Santa Fe had promised and thirteen hours faster than the regular Santa Fe Limited's time.

Scotty claimed that the trip cost him $100,000. Actually, he paid the Santa Fe $5,500, which is about as close as Walter Scott of Death Valley usually came to the truth. Why did he go to such expense and bother to make the trip? For publicity, the thing he loved above everything else. And it wasn't even his own money. Eventually the truth about Death Valley Scotty came out. He didn't have a gold mine, never had had. He did have an "angel," however, a wealthy retired Chicago businessman named Albert M. Johnson who put up the money for Scotty's stunts and his fantastic castle. Years later Johnson admitted, "Scotty doesn't have a dime that he can call his own. I've been paying Scotty's bills for years, and I like it. He repays me in laughs." As for the Coyote Special, everybody had fun, except the passenger who foolishly tried to stand up in the aisle when the train was careening around a curve at high speed and was thrown against the side of the car so hard that his shoulder broke a window.

Less exciting than Scotty's private train but far more important were the "whistle stop" trains in which candidates for election as President of the United States campaigned around the country. Today a candidate in a chartered airplane can make a breakfast campaign appearance on the East Coast, deliver two or three speeches at Midwestern and Southwestern cities during the day, and appear in Los Angeles that evening at a nationally televised rally. Within a single day he has shown himself to voters from coast to coast. In the days before jetliners and television, the Presidential candidate traveled the same route by private train and took days to do it.

The campaign train was a special world on wheels. At each stop the candidate stepped onto the open observation platform and made a short speech, frequently the same one with just the

Design of observation car with ten sections. Other types combined drawing rooms, compartments, bedrooms, and sun rooms.

local town name changed, to whatever crowd gathered along the tracks. Perhaps only a hundred people showed up, perhaps several thousand. While he was speaking, local politicians were invited aboard the train to ride to the next town. On the way, the candidate chatted with them and made them feel important.

Dozens of reporters rode on the train. At each halt they scrambled to the ground and gathered at the rear to see if by chance the candidate said anything new. Occasionally one of them who tarried too long was surprised to see the train pull out without him. Western Union had a representative aboard to collect the press stories and drop them off at telegraph stations along the way. Whenever the campaign party stopped overnight in a large city, reporters and politicians alike headed for hotel rooms. It was their only opportunity to take a bath.

Because politicians love to talk, keeping a back platform whistle-stop candidate's train on time was a problem for the trainmaster. One of the worst offenders was William Jennings Bryan. Often the trainmaster ordered the train to pull out while Bryan was still talking to the receding crowd. With his booming voice, he could be heard quite a distance down the track.

Presidential campaign trains have disappeared into history, except when a candidate uses one occasionally for a few hours in a special area. President Harry S Truman made a most famous whistle-stop campaign in 1948, when he was fighting to win a full term in the White House. As Vice President, he had become President in 1945 after President Franklin D. Roosevelt died. His Truman Special of sixteen cars traveled 25,000 miles up and down the country. Aboard were a hundred news reporters, speech writers, political assistants, Secret Service men, secretaries, and Western Union men. On some days Mr. Truman made as many as twenty speeches. After talking from the back platform under a

President Harry S Truman makes a brief whistle stop speech at an Indiana farm town during his 1948 campaign tour. Henry F. Schricker, the successful candidate for governor of Indiana, stands beside him.

Throng assembles outside the Union Station at South Bend, Indiana, to hear President Truman during his 1948 whistle stop campaign tour. Truman stands between the observation car and the bunting-covered railing at the far left.

canvas awning for a few minutes, he leaned over the rail to shake hands with those he could reach. He was still shaking hands as the train pulled out. At times during the day, his motorcade dashed from the train station behind police sirens to a downtown platform, where he spoke for a few minutes, then sped back to the train. It was this relentless train traveling around the country, with the opportunity it gave him to be seen up close by six million Americans, that helped Mr. Truman squeeze out a victory over Thomas E. Dewey when most political experts thought he would lose.

Gaudiest and most fascinating of all the special trains that once rolled along American rails were the circus trains.

This was in the era when circuses performed in gigantic tents on vacant lots in cities, rather than in air-conditioned indoor arenas, as most of them do now. Many fans who remember those days claim that the real spirit of the "big top" died when circuses moved indoors.

At the close of the evening performance under canvas, roustabouts already were at work "knocking down" the circus, even before the last of the audience had left the sawdust area. Tent ropes were loosened, the huge brown canvas tent was lowered and folded, and the sideshows closed. Lions and tigers were prodded into the heavily barred red and gold menagerie wagons. The elephants twined their trunks around the massive main tent poles and other pieces of heavy equipment and hauled them to waiting vans. Within two or three hours the entire circus was loaded aboard a train for an overnight ride to the next city.

A circus train was a mixed bag of cars—Pullman sleepers for the performers, baggage cars, and flatcars loaded with the animal wagons and tents.

The next morning in another city the excitement began anew. For days garish posters had announced the circus's coming. Hundreds of people gathered to watch the circus train unload, marveling at the precision of the operation. Clowns emerged from the Pullmans in their outlandish costumes. The tigers in their caged wagons snarled. The elephants were lined up single file, each holding the tail of the animal ahead with its trunk. While

Photo shows unloading of a Barnum & Bailey circus train in 1908.

A circus family featured in the 1976 Bicentennial Edition of Ringling Bros. and Barnum & Bailey Circus travels in a modern circus train.

the steam calliope shrieked a tune, the circus parade marched from the train to the grounds where the performance was to be held that afternoon. The town was a-tingle with anticipation.

The elephants on a circus train traveling on the Gulf Lines in Texas got it into a strange mishap, and then rescued it. The train had been switched onto a siding to wait for a passenger train to pass. Three elephants being transported on the front car stuck their trunks into the water tank of the engine tender ahead of them, sucked up the water, and had a delightful time giving themselves showers. Sheer elephant delight in the sticky Texas weather! With no water left to raise steam, the train was stalled on the siding. So the locomotive was uncoupled, the elephants were unloaded, and the giant beasts towed the locomotive three miles down the track for refilling.

One circus train never reached its destination. The Hagenback-Wallace Circus was among the biggest and finest in operation in 1918, at the peak of World War I. On the night of June 22 the show finished its performance at Michigan City, Indiana, and was loaded aboard two trains for an overnight trip to Hammond. Making up the second train were fourteen flatcars, seven animal cars, four old wooden Pullman sleeping cars, and a caboose.

The Pullmans in which the performers slept were dingy left-

". . . the startled flagman saw a train's headlight bearing down on him. . . ."

overs from earlier times. They had three tiers of berths. Dim oil lamps hanging in the aisle gave the cars skimpy illumination.

Among those asleep in these cars were the boss clown, the star woman bareback rider, the strong man, and the dancing girls of Hagenback-Wallace's 100-member ballet. Shortly before dawn, a trainman thought he smelled a hotbox on the axle of one car and ordered the train stopped for inspection. A flagman was sent back down the track with a lantern to protect the train's rear, in usual railroad fashion. The line also had automatic signal warning lights.

Suddenly the startled flagman saw a train's headlight bearing down on him at high speed. He waved his lantern wildly and as the engine passed him, tossed an explosive warning torpedo at the engineer's cab. The onrushing train, an empty troop train of heavy steel cars, didn't slow down even a trifle. Like a clap of thunder it smashed into the rear of the standing circus train.

The wreckage and chaos that followed were appalling. Mingled with the roars of terrified animals were the screams of the performers trapped in the shattered wooden cars. The oil lamps were knocked loose and set the Pullmans afire. Soon the circus train became a towering torch whose flames could be seen for miles. When daylight came, the scattered debris made a pitiful sight—spangled clothing, tinsel decorations, other charred remnants of circus equipment. Survivors sat on the ground, moaning or in silent shock. Many of the suffering animals had to be shot. Sixty-eight circus people died in the smashup.

An investigation disclosed that the engineer of the troop train had taken medicine that made him drowsy. He had fallen asleep at the throttle, so that he had not seen either the yellow caution signal or the red stop signal. Nor had he heard the warning torpedo. His fireman was so busy shoveling coal into the speeding train's firebox that he hadn't been aware of the warnings. It was the worst circus train wreck in history.

7

TWENTY MINUTES FOR DINNER

A tousle-headed young man pushed through the door at the front of the railroad coach, carrying a deep tray fastened to his front by a leather strap around his neck.

"Candy! Peanuts! Apples!" he called out.

Every passenger in the car looked up, except the few who had fallen asleep to the rhythmic clicking sound of the car wheels rolling over the joints in the steel rails. The young man moved along the car, halting at every seat to peddle his wares. Frequently he made a sale, providing refreshment for the passengers and a profit for himself. He disappeared into the car behind, only to reappear a bit later with his tray empty, on his way forward to his supply base in the baggage car up front.

Less than a half hour later he repeated his journey, this time selling soft drinks. Just enough time had elapsed for the passengers to become thirsty from the peanuts and candy.

On his third trip he offered magazines and paperback books for sale. Some riders made selections from his varied reading wares immediately. Others fussed and dawdled, unable to make up their minds. With the skill of a clever salesman, the young man handed a hesitating passenger a magazine he thought she would enjoy, saying, "Here, read this while I go through the train. If you don't like it, I'll pick it up on my way back." Usually when he returned, the passenger was deep into a story and paid for the magazine, rather than have to quit reading in the middle.

The young man was a news butcher. He had exclusive rights to sell merchandise on the train and divided his profits with the railroad company. This enterprising breed of young salesmen has disappeared from modern trains, but in earlier years they were a commonplace sight on most daytime runs. Many men of earlier generations got their start on successful careers as news butchers. The most famous of these was Thomas A. Edison, who was to become the United States' most renowned inventor.

Young Tom became a train news vendor when he was only thirteen, on a Grand Trunk mixed passenger and freight train between his home in Port Huron, Michigan, and Detroit. Nobody paid much attention to attending school in those days. That was in 1860, just before the Civil War. Tom was an ambitious youth who didn't want to waste a minute of his time. In addition to making sales trips through the coaches, he put a small printing press in the baggage car and published his own newspaper, *The Herald*, for sale to the passengers. Not only local items but national and foreign news appeared in its columns. The latter he obtained from friendly telegraph operators at stations along the route.

Even that wasn't enough to keep him occupied on the long, slow trips. He built a small chemistry laboratory in the baggage car, too, and did experiments on the way.

The deafness that afflicted Edison most of his life began while he was a news butcher. He was trying to climb into a freight car with an armload of newspapers, and a trainman helped him by pulling him up by the ears. Something snapped in Tom's head, impairing his hearing.

Edison's career as a news butcher ended suddenly. When he was doing an experiment in his rolling laboratory, a stick of phosphorus set the wooden baggage car afire. The angry conductor threw Tom and his equipment off the train.

Dining cars were carried on relatively few trains except the fast "through trains" or expresses about which the railroads boasted. Even on some trains that had them, coach passengers hesitated to go into the diners because they thought the meals cost too much.

An *early-day dining car, depicted by a* Harper's Magazine *artist*

A sketch of busy dining car interior

They either brought along their own meals and ate them in their seats or depended on the news butcher to sell fruit, candy, and sandwiches. On hundreds of local trains puttering along from one city to another without pretensions of being glamorous, the butcher was the only source of refreshment.

For several decades after the first transcontinental route was completed, trains on the long Western run had no dining car service. Instead, they stopped for meal breaks three times a day, to allow the passengers to get off and hurry into a trackside restaurant for a hasty meal.

Usually, but not always, the restaurant was in the railroad station. Trains on the old Minneapolis & St. Louis Railroad stopped in one town on the route, and passengers paraded across the street to a hotel dining room. At remote points where no restaurants existed, local townspeople met the trains with dinners packed in market baskets which they sold to the passengers for fifty cents.

It was common practice for a trainman to ask passengers how

Passengers from an early-day train hurry into a railroad-station lunch counter for a quick meal while the train waits. A painting by H. D. Stitt.

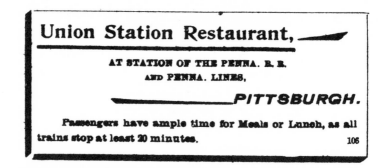

An old ad for a station restaurant

many wanted dinner at the approaching meal stop. He wired the total ahead, and that many meals were prepared for the arriving travelers.

When the train stopped, the conductor called, "Twenty minutes for dinner!" The stampede to the dining room was on.

Railroad station food had a reputation for being terrible, a reputation well deserved. The restaurant operators knew they had a captive audience, most of whom would never pass that way again. So they dished up cold, poorly cooked food and told the passengers to like it or go hungry. Railroad restaurant pie was in particularly bad repute. Its crust tasted like cardboard and the filling seemingly was held together with glue. The doughnuts were as bad. The only fresh part of them was the hole. Having to gulp down the food before the train whistle blew and the conductor shouted "All aboard!" didn't help the digestion. Sometimes a practical joker stuck his head into the restaurant and shouted "All aboard!" too soon, just to see the eaters scramble.

On some lines, hungry passengers were trapped in a plot between restaurant owners and train crews. The passengers paid fifty cents in advance for their meals. No sooner had they been seated and started to eat than the locomotive bell rang. Not wanting to be left behind, they dashed back to the train, leaving their almost untouched meals to be scraped onto new plates, reheated, and served to the next trainload. The restaurant owner paid off the cooperative trainmen with ten cents for each passenger "served."

Fred Harvey changed all that, at least along the two thousand miles of the Santa Fe Railroad between Chicago and Los Angeles.

Back in 1876, Harvey, a freight agent, proposed to the Santa Fe that if the railroad would back him, he would open a good quality restaurant that wouldn't cheat the passengers. He bought a dingy restaurant in the Topeka, Kansas, station. Harvey closed the restaurant for two days. He scrubbed it, dressed up the tables with tablecloths and napkins, laid out polished silver, and opened up to serve good food at a reasonable price. Soon he was doing capacity business. Next he bought a broken-down trackside hotel in the town of Florence, Kansas. Not only did he adorn the dining room with Irish linen and English silver but he installed elaborate walnut furniture in the hotel rooms—this in a remote prairie town with a population of a hundred persons! To add a final touch of class, he hired a chef from the elite Palmer House in Chicago to operate the railroad restaurant.

The fame of the Florence hotel and restaurant spread up and down the Santa Fe. Passengers flocked in when the train made a meal stop at Florence, and many stayed overnight in the little

The wild rush of passengers back from a station lunchroom as their train prepares to depart. Food is scattered on the platform, in this Currier & Ives print.

Harvey Girls wait at the lunch counter in Deming, New Mexico, for a train to arrive (1901).

community to enjoy the novelty of splendid accomodations and food in such an isolated spot. Fred Harvey was on his way.

His greatest stroke of business skill was organizing the Harvey Girls. This was the corps of waitresses who served in Harvey's expanding string of Santa Fe station restaurants. They became known throughout the West, indeed across the entire country. Harvey and the Santa Fe recruited them by advertising in Eastern and Midwestern newspapers for "Young women of good character, attractive and intelligent, 18 to 30." Hundreds of young women anxious for adventure in the West applied. They promised not to marry until they had been on the job at least a year.

At each town where Harvey Girls were stationed, they lived in a dormitory under the supervision of a matron and had to be in by ten o'clock at night. Their pay and tips were excellent but their lives were closely regulated. Strict rules of dress on the job were enforced. The girls wore long black uniforms with white collars and white ribbons in their hair, giving them a demure air.

Harvey's restaurants were arranged to serve masses of hungry train passengers in the shortest possible amount of time. Travelers could have either lunch-counter service for light snacks or full dinners. Those who desired dinner received identical food, to eliminate the delays caused by individual order taking. When the train still was miles from the station, the conductor polled the passengers and telegraphed ahead to say how many persons wanted each type of service.

A mile from the station, the Santa Fe engineer blew the locomotive whistle. A Harvey Girl outside the station banged the dinner gong once, the signal for the other waitresses to place the first course of the meal on the tables. As the train stopped, the clattering gong called the passengers into the depot restaurant.

Harvey insisted that his patrons dress with dignity. If a passenger in shirtsleeves entered the restaurant, a Harvey Girl stopped him politely.

"I'm sorry, sir, you must wear a coat to be served," she ex-

The first Santa Fe passenger train to reach Albuquerque, New Mexico, raises a cloud of black smoke as it enters town in 1880. Travelers were always glad to find a Fred Harvey restaurant at the depot.

plained. She handed him a black jacket from a supply on a nearby rack. He returned it when he left. Thus did Harvey maintain decorum in the rough-and-ready era of the West. Even the coatless travelers who had been clothed in this manner were impressed by this stylish demand.

As soon as the diners were settled in their places and started on their first course, a Harvey Girl asked each what he or she wanted to drink—coffee, tea, iced tea, or milk. Moments later the "drink girl" came along and poured the desired liquids without hesitation. She knew unerringly what each customer wanted.

This trick was accomplished by use of Harvey's private cup code. Upon hearing the customer's desire, the first waitress had moved the cup into a certain position. A cup left right-side-up in the saucer meant coffee, upside down meant hot tea, upside down but tilted against the saucer meant iced tea, and upside down away from the saucer meant milk.

While the drinks were being served, the manager emerged from the kitchen carrying a tray heaped with the main course, and the girls distributed the laden plates. Within two or three minutes after the train had stopped, scores of passengers were eating busily. Split-second timing and organization made it possible for the travelers to dine at a comfortable pace, without being forced to gulp their meals, and to finish before the warning bell of the locomotive tolled its signal.

For many Harvey Girls, the railroad restaurant jobs were the path to romance. Much as airline stewardesses do today, the girls sometimes married passengers they met on the job. Others became wives of trainmen and prominent local citizens. In Western towns where men heavily outnumbered women, these attractive young Eastern girls drew numerous suitors. Knowing human nature as he did, Harvey wasn't surprised that Harvey Girls often didn't wait a year to marry, despite their pledge. In fact, he staged parties for the newlyweds at times. His methods were so successful that when he died in 1901, he and the Santa Fe owned and operated a string of fifteen hotels, forty-seven restaurants, and thirty dining cars, plus a San Francisco Bay ferry.

Before automobiles and good roads were common, railroad ex-

Two Santa Fe stations—at Belen and Clovis, New Mexico—offer food.

cursions on weekends and holidays were America's way of having fun. Special excursion trains with reduced price tickets ran into the big cities from rural areas, giving the country folks an opportunity to see the bright lights. When great events like the Chicago Columbian Exposition of 1893 or the St. Louis Exposition a few years later were staged, scores of thousands of sight-seers jammed the trains to visit the shows on special bargain tickets.

Excursion trains traveled outbound from the cities, too, carrying urban holiday-makers on one-day or weekend tours to resorts and renowned natural attractions such as Niagara Falls. How

During the Gay Nineties, special trains carried holiday-makers on excursions to beach resorts such as the Redondo Hotel and Bath House on the Pacific Ocean shore of Southern California.

many young couples were married in the cities, then took honeymoon trips to the Falls on cut-priced tickets will never be known, but they numbered in the thousands every year. Niagara Falls became known as the Honeymoon Capital of the United States.

Some railroads offered special rates to nowhere in particular. The Nickel Plate Railroad, for example, during the 1890's in Ohio, permitted a group of five persons to travel anywhere up to one hundred miles, then home again the same day, for one dollar each on Sundays.

A typical Gay Nineties excursion was the one run by the Western Maryland Railroad from Baltimore to the Pen-Mar Resort in the Blue Ridge mountains, seventy-one miles away. This resort existed only because of these excursions, because reaching it by horse and buggy, the only other common way of traveling at that time, was difficult.

When the train left Baltimore on Sunday morning, it was thronged by women in ankle-length dresses and men in business suits with high stiff collars, neckties, and broad-brimmed straw hats. Holiday-makers in that era didn't dream of the comfort in clothing that we have today. Men couldn't buy sports shirts, and for a woman to appear in a short skirt or—heaven forbid!—a pair of shorts would have made everyone on the Sunday School picnic blush. On a hot summer day, with windows open to let fresh air into the coaches and cinders into the eyes of the passengers, the crowd began to wilt before it reached the mountain resort. Many carried lunches in cloth-covered baskets, to be eaten picnic-style after arrival. Bored, hungry children tried to wheedle their mothers into opening the baskets early, usually without success.

Once at Pen-Mar, there really wasn't much entertainment for the visitors. Piling from the trains that pulled in rows onto sidings to await the return trip that evening, the day-trippers admired the mountain scenery and walked along paths through the woods. They sat in rocking chairs on the broad porches of the hotels, fanning themselves in the heat. No swimming pool existed, and no air conditioning. They opened their picnic baskets or dined on fifty-cent chicken dinners in the restaurants. The most exciting amusement at Pen-Mar for children was riding on the miniature railroad.

Perhaps it sounds like a dull way to spend Sunday, but the people of that time didn't think so. They demanded less in the way of formal entertainment than we do today, and for those who worked six ten-hour days a week in a factory, a Sunday train ride into the mountains was a delightful change.

Young couples in particular found the excursions romantic. Knowing this, the Knights of Columbus advertised their outing to Pen-Mar this way: "Bring your intended. Pen-Mar has lots of places where you can pop the question without fear of distur-bance. If her family is the kind that parks in the parlor every time you call, this is your opportunity."

The train trip up to the resort was alive with noisy chatter and anticipation. Not so the return trip. By then, everyone was hot, dusty, weary, and subdued. The miles seemed to drag on endlessly. Once the train arrived at the Baltimore station, most of the holiday-makers had to take a streetcar ride before they reached their homes, and perhaps walk a few blocks after leaving the streetcar. They were worn out but convinced that they had had a good time.

High up in the Rocky Mountains, another kind of excursion became popular some years later along the narrow gauge route of the almost forgotten Denver, South Park, and Pacific Railroad. This was a fisherman's delight. The tracks twisted southwest through the mountains from Denver to Leadville, crossing over the Continental Divide twice on the way. The third time the train reached the Divide, it went through a tunnel at an altitude of 11,596 feet. The little locomotive huffed and puffed to get its string of cars through these lofty altitudes but rarely broke down.

The railroad was the principal way for guests to reach many mountain resorts, such as this one at Shasta Springs, California, in 1897.

Narrow gauge tracks often could be laid where construction of regulation width tracks was not practical because of narrow spaces in mountain canyons and on ledges high up on cliff slopes.

The D, SP and P track ran through Platte Canyon on the South Platte River, renowned for its good fishing. Thus were born the railroad's "fish trains." On the way out from Denver, as the train crawled along, a fisherman passenger would select a spot and ask the conductor to stop the train. The conductor pulled the bell cord and the engineer, getting the signal, slowed to a halt. The fisherman got off, unloaded his rods and overnight camping equipment, and cast his line into the swift, tumbling water. As the train moved ahead in stop-and-start jerks, it disgorged scores of fishermen. The next morning the train made the return trip. When they heard its whistle and saw the train approaching, the fishermen waved handkerchiefs to signal the engineer to stop and pick them up. Their creels were full of Rocky Mountain trout, their hearts were happy, and the air in the coaches was laced with the pungent odor of fish. Many a family in Denver had a pan full of fresh trout for dinner that night.

Most small railroads such as the D, SP and P that snaked through the mountains into remote areas, hauling out timber and ore, have gone out of existence. At one time these narrow tracks and scaled-down trains were the only form of transportation into thinly populated mountain areas. When snowstorms blocked the tracks, people in the isolated camps and villages had to manage without fresh supplies from the outside world. The opening of roads has made hauling by truck more efficient. Logs that had been carried out from the forests on flatcars now are borne in huge lumber trucks that sound like express trains coming down the twisting mountain roads in low gear. But a few narrow gauge railroads still operate at least part of the year, and in summer run passenger trains filled with nostalgia seekers and camera enthusiasts.

One of these in Northern California is known as the Skunk. The strange name was coined forty years ago because the train consisted of one car with a gasoline engine that gave off a stench. This little train runs forty miles from Fort Bragg on the Pacific

Railway to a lumber camp

Coast through the mountains to Willits, in an inland valley, over the California Western logging railroad. At night, heavy logging trains run over the California Western line, bringing timber down to the sawmill at Fort Bragg.

The Skunk leaves Fort Bragg in the morning, meandering through heavy forest up the Noyo River Valley to Willits, and returns after lunch. On the morning trip, the crew picks up grocery orders placed by isolated residents in boxes alongside the track. The trainmen purchase the groceries in Willits, and on the return trip make frequent stops to deliver the supplies into the trackside boxes. On one such trip, made by this writer, the Skunk was forced to halt in a mountain tunnel because a cow was trotting along the track through the darkened bore ahead of the train. While the train crept behind it, the animal moved slowly along the track toward daylight, its udder swinging and cowbell clanging. Train schedules meant nothing to it. There was no way to tell whether it had blundered into the tunnel by accident or had discovered an easy, level shortcut that saved it from having to climb over a mountain ridge.

Then there is the Rocky Mountain Mud Hen, a narrow gauge

100

passenger train running in the Rockies each summer from Durango, Colorado, up to the little mining town of Silverton along forty-five miles of track that twists through breath-taking mountain gorges and over bridges high above the swift Animas River. This train with its old-style, coal-burning steam locomotives and narrow yellow passenger coaches is straight out of the distant past. So many people want to ride it that reservations must be made in advance for the daily excursion. At one point the train crawls along a right-of-way only five feet wide, hacked from a granite cliff five hundred feet above the foaming river. At other points, the track is so close to the water that passengers feel as though they almost can reach out the windows and dip their hands in the chill, clear liquid.

Just as in the old days, the train reaches the end of the track at Silverton, which has changed little in three quarters of a century. Passengers pile out for lunch in the old-fashioned Imperial Hotel and nearby eating houses, then go aboard again for the afternoon trip back down the mountain to Durango. Except for the travelers' modern clothing and the abundance of cameras, the excursion train is just like the ones our great-great grandparents rode back in the Nineties.

101

8

SWIFT TRAINS AND SLOW

As railroad tracks were made heavier and roadbeds stronger in the last part of the 1800's, passenger trains could go faster. The railroads began to put catchy names like Thunderbolt, Cannonball, Hummer, and even G-whiz-z on the trains to make them sound more exciting, although in fact most trains in the 1880's still ran at about forty miles an hour. Even that speed was so much faster than any other form of transportation that passengers didn't feel cheated.

Then the New York Central caught the attention of the country, causing onlookers to exclaim, "My heavens!" It ran the country's first heavy, high-speed train across the State of New York from New York City to Buffalo. This train was named, appropriately enough, the Empire State Express. To dramatize it, the New York Central built a special locomotive, Number 999, to pull the shiny line of varnished coaches. In May, 1893, engineer Charlie Hogan opened Engine 999's throttle all the way on a stretch of track west of Batavia, New York, on the run from Syracuse to Buffalo, and the Empire State Express covered a mile at the spectacular speed of 112.5 miles an hour. The nation was amazed.

That was the year the Columbian Exposition opened in Chicago. Engine 999 and the Empire State Express were put on display at the exposition, under the gaze of sight-seeing throngs who marveled that anything could go so fast. The train was pic-

The World's Fair Buildings, Chicago. The New York Central's new name train, the Empire State Express, was put on display at the 1893 Columbian Exposition there.

tured on a two-cent U.S. postage stamp commemorating the Exposition. That is all it cost to mail a first class letter in those days.

Alas for Engine 999, however, she proved to be more a sprinter than a long-distance runner, fleet afoot but unable to haul a heavy load. Having had her moment of glory, she was taken off the Empire State Express and replaced by a slower, stronger locomotive. Her wheels were cut down in size and she was assigned to less flamboyant jobs. Soon she was forgotten. Years later old 999 was rediscovered, pulling a dreary milk train at a crawl between Watertown and Carthage, New York. The New York Central restored her to original form and put her on display for show occasions.

In her day, the Empire State Express was the wonder of railroading—the first train to have enclosed vestibules instead of open-ended coaches, and the first to have steps that folded up when the doors closed, in a primitive form of streamlining.

This train was eclipsed by an even more glamorous one on the same railroad, when the Central inaugurated the Twentieth Century Limited between New York and Chicago in 1903. Other railroads developed star trains, too. Among them were the Golden State Limited, the Wabash Cannonball, the Panama Limited, the Red Arrow, the Chief, the Lark, the Oriental Limited, the Flying Yankee, and the Black Diamond Express. Soon the country

Northern Pacific's name train, the North Coast Limited, made its first trip from the Midwest to the Pacific Coast in 1900. It was the first electrically-lighted train on that run and introduced steam heat, baths, and barber-valet service to Northwest travelers.

was crisscrossed with these proud, swift expresses laying down streaks of smoke as they sped between cities, day and night.

These fast trains carried Railway Mail Service cars up front next to the baggage cars. These traveling post offices were manned by staffs of mail clerks who sorted mail as the train sped along, thus hurrying up delivery at the other end. Stacks of loaded canvas mailbags were piled on the car when it started. Racks of open-mouthed mailbags lined the center of the car, each marked with a destination. The clerks opened the loaded bags, sorted their contents according to destination, and tossed the letters into the proper sacks on the rack. Bracing themselves as the train swayed around curves, the men worked on through the night. As bags on the rack were filled, they were tied and sealed by the time the train reached its destination, where they were sent to the post office in trucks or wagons for local delivery, or were transferred to other trains that would carry them to their final destination. Delivery of letters was speeded immensely by the railroad mail cars.

The most exciting part of the Railway Mail Service was picking up mailbags on the fly as the express train raced through small towns without stopping. A metal arm on hinges was swung out from the side of the mail car. The local station agent hung his bag of outgoing mail on an elevated rack alongside the track. When the train raced past, the arm snatched the bag from the rack. A clerk pulled in the arm, detached the bag, and tossed it on the stack for sorting. Mailbags addressed to the town were thrown out the open door of the car onto the platform. Tossing a mailbag from a speeding train so it would land precisely at the proper spot on the platform took as much skill as swishing a basketball through a net with a twenty-foot jump shot.

Among railroad men there is a story about a mail clerk in Nebraska whose keychain became entangled in a mail sack as he

Railway Mail Service car and smoker combination

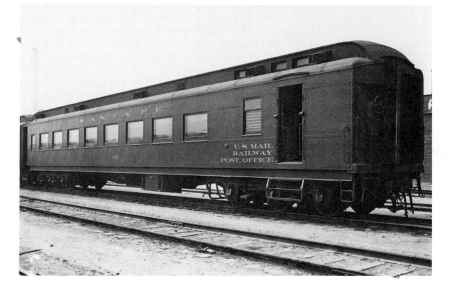

threw it out, dragging him out the door, too. He grabbed the pickup arm extending from the side of the car and hung on for his life until other clerks pulled him in.

The Pennsylvania Railroad, arch competitor of the New York Central until the two lines eventually were combined into the Penn Central, developed a fleet of "name" trains that was perhaps the most extensive in the country. The Broadway Limited was the rival of the Twentieth Century Limited on the New York-Chicago run, matching luxury with luxury, speed with speed. In the early days when the Broadway Limited was known as the Pennsylvania Special, it set a startling speed record of 127.1 miles an hour along a three-mile stretch of track in Western Ohio.

At the peak of the passenger train era in the 1920's and 1930's, railroad enthusiasts who perched themselves near the Pennsy's renowned Horseshoe Curve between Harrisburg and Pittsburgh, Pennsylvania, at night saw a sight that never will be duplicated. In a period of five hours between 10:43 P.M. and 3:41 A.M. daily, twenty-seven "name" trains—the General, the Trail Blazer, the

Catching the mail sack as a train passed through a town could be dangerous.

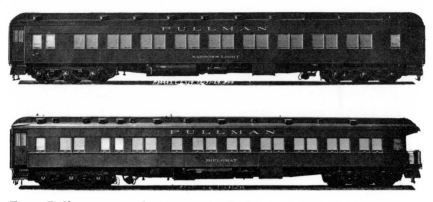

Every Pullman car on the name trains had its own name.

Manhattan Limited, the Spirit of St. Louis, and others that long since have gone out of existence and whose names are almost forgotten—rounded the curve. Headlights splitting the night, sparks dancing from smokestacks and brakes, scattered lights gleaming in the darkened Pullmans, the trains sped to various destinations from the East Coast to the Mississippi River.

Every Pullman car on those trains had its own name. Since there were hundreds of such cars, finding enough names was a problem. Sometimes the results were quite a mouthful. Some carried the names of men famous in history. Others had place names from around the United States, among them some so remote that the committee of Pullman Company officials who did the naming must have searched the geography books with a magnifying glass. Also, the committee dug into Greek and Roman mythology, where they found such names as *Circe, Archimedes,* and *Belisarius.* A passenger walking from Pullman to Pullman always wondered what unexpected name would greet him at each door.

The sounds of speeding passenger trains fascinated even those who rarely rode on them. For years the Louisville & Nashville Railroad, recognizing this, used the sounds of its fast southbound Pan American as a daily radio advertisement. Each afternoon a microphone from station WSM in Nashville, Tennessee, was placed alongside the L&N tracks as the Pan American approached. Listeners could hear the high, shrill whistle of the distant train,

107

then the gathering roar as it thundered past, its wheels vibrating over the rail points *clackety, clackety, clack.* Slowly the sounds diminished as the train vanished in the distance, until only the fading whistle could be heard. Thousands of persons made it a point to listen every day, carried away in their minds to distant places by the sounds. Some became so expert that they could identify different engineers on the Pan American by their touch on its whistle and could tell the number of cars on the train each day by counting the clicks of the wheels.

When train travel reached its highest point in the United States, twenty thousand regularly scheduled passenger trains were running. Not all of them could be glamorous trains with express schedules. For every such star, there were a score of plodding local trains that stopped at every station. Since little towns every ten miles or so had stations, this meant frequent stops and often long waits while parcels, mail sacks, crates, and baggage were loaded and unloaded. Usually the late night train along each route, known as the milk train, took aboard cans of milk, brought by farmers direct from their barnyards to the station, for early morning delivery in the nearest large city. It even stopped at designated road crossings in the country to pick up cans. In some farm towns this train was nicknamed "the milk shake."

Unlike today's air terminals, which are located at the far edge of cities, railroad stations were right downtown. This made them community gathering places. Going down to the station—or depot, as it was usually called, using the French word but mispronouncing it "dee-po"—to watch the train stop was favorite entertainment in small towns. You could see who was arriving and leaving and secretly wish that you, too, were climbing aboard the cars. Or even better, aboard the locomotive to ride with the engineer and fireman. A few of the town's loafers usually hung around the platform, sitting on the wooden baggage trucks with their legs dangling over the side. Boys put pennies on the track for the train to run over. When they picked up the coins later, the weight of the locomotive and cars had squashed them thin and two or three times their original size.

108

Station on the Chicago and North Western Railway, located at Canal and Kinzie Streets, Chicago, 1848. Depots were located in the center of towns.

Waiting on the platform for the train to arrive stirred the blood and the imagination—peering up the track time after time, seeing nothing. Then came the faraway sound of the whistle as the engineer blew a warning for the crossroad two miles away . . . the sudden appearance of a headlight beam on the horizon, growing bigger every moment . . . another whistle blast, much louder . . . the locomotive slowing to a stop as it passed the station, steam hissing and bell ringing. A good engineer could halt the train so the baggage car doors were directly in line with the waiting baggage wagon on the platform.

A few minutes later, with baggage and passengers loaded, the train pulled slowly away and disappeared around a curve. The station telegrapher went back to his chattering key, the arriving passengers loaded their luggage into waiting vehicles, and the loafers drifted back to a card game. A little bit of the outer world had come and gone.

At one little town far out in the California desert, the loafers had a stunt to amaze the passengers. In summer, desert temperatures often reach 115 degrees Fahrenheit in the shade. There wasn't much shade around the old wooden depot. Nor did the cars have air conditioning. When the Southern Pacific train from

Watching the train arrive in a cloud of steam was always exciting, and the waiting van, drawn by a team of horses, was a welcome sight to early-day travelers, in Kansas and elsewhere.

the East stopped for a few minutes, perspiring passengers stepped onto the platform in search of a cooling breeze. There wasn't any.

"Say, how hot is it here, anyway?" at least one passenger invariably would ask.

"About 140," a loafer would reply.

"It can't be that hot."

"Sure it is. Look at that thermometer on the station wall."

The passenger looked, saw the mercury hitting the top of the tube, and hurried back onto the train, thinking that it had to be cooler aboard. He didn't know that the local wags had held a match under the thermometer ball a few moments before the train arrived.

Aboard the day coaches of those local trains rode a mixed lot of passengers—traveling salesmen with their heavy sample cases, going from town to town selling their wares to merchants; women traveling on family visits; small town residents on their way to the county seat for a day of shopping; children from the little communities riding to high school in the nearby larger town. Since

110

many were regular riders and the train crews often were local people, the conductors and passengers came to know each other. An air of friendly informality developed.

"Good morning, Mrs. Stewart. Going to Richmond?" The conductor took her ticket and made holes in it with his hand punch, the little snippets of paper falling to the car floor.

"Yes, I'm doing my Christmas shopping. I'll be back on the 4:15 in time to make Will's dinner."

The conductor pushed a yellow cardboard slip, punched to show that she was riding to the end of the train's run, under a brass clip on the back of the green velour seat.

"How is your daughter's baby? She must be talking by now."

"Talking like a streak, thank you."

That's the way life was on the local runs.

Up forward behind the locomotive was the smoking car. Usually it was a combination car, the front half a baggage compartment and the back half for passengers. This was a man's world exclusively, its air stuffy with the smoke of cigars and pipes. Men played cards on wooden tables set up between the seats. They propped their feet on the cushions, argued politics, and told yarns.

Since the passengers on smoking cars usually seemed to include a few railroad men "deadheading"—riding free, that is—the stories often were about railroading. The slowness of trains was a favorite topic. The stories were told as though they had happened on a certain railroad; the same stories were heard elsewhere in the country, supposedly having happened on quite a different line. For some reason, Southern railroads seemed to be the butt of many such jokes.

One was about a train in Arkansas that the storyteller claimed was the slowest he ever saw. "It stopped at every house. When it came to a double house, it stopped twice. They made so many stops I said, 'What have we stopped for now?'

"The conductor said, 'There are some cattle on the track.'

"We ran a little farther and stopped again. I said, 'What is it now?'

"He replied, 'We've caught up with those cattle again.'"

111

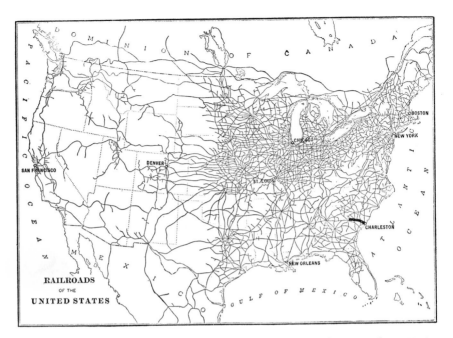

Map compares first railroad at Charleston in 1830 with network of 1903.

Pullman porters were the object of stories that the tellers claimed were true, and perhaps some of them were. One is about a porter who collected the shoes of his sleeping passengers to shine. Although it was against the rules for him to leave his car, he decided to do his work in the next Pullman with its porter, so he would have someone to talk to during the long night hours. He carried the pile of shoes with him.

Starting back to his own car some time later, he was startled to discover that at the last stop it had been cut out of the train and transferred to the second section following fifteen minutes later. If he was upset, think of his passengers who had to get off the train without shoes the next morning!

Another favorite about porters concerned the passenger who boarded a New York Central train at Buffalo, New York, one night and told the porter that he was to be sworn in as a member of the state legislature at Albany the next day.

"I've got to be there," he said. "Even if I'm asleep and in my pajamas, don't fail to put me off the train when we arrive in Albany."

The porter promised.

The next morning the train pulled into Grand Central Terminal in New York, still carrying the would-be legislator. He was furious when he discovered where he was and ran from the Pullman into the station in his pajamas, swearing unstatesmanlike oaths. The porter hid behind a post.

Another porter asked him, "What's the matter with that man running in his pajamas? Is he mad!"

"He sure is. But nothing compared to the man I put off at Albany."

Even when timetables were "jokes," they were a source of fascination; now, with new routes being added, they're invitations to adventure. Amtrak offers dining and dome cars on the Albany-Montreal run.

The Adirondack

Operates Daily/Quotidien

★69	Miles Milles	Type of Service/Service	★68
10 00a	0	Dp.............**NEW YORK, NY**⊙.............Ar (Grand Central Terminal/gare Grand Central)	8 00p
r10 50a	33	Ar ⎰.............Croton-Harmon⊙.............⎰ Dp	d 7 07p
r10 57a	33	Dp ⎱ ⎱ Ar	d 7 00p
r11 40a	73	.........Poughkeepsie⊙ (*Highland*).........	d 6 14p
11 55a	88	.............Rhinecliff (*Kingston*).............	5 59p
12 17p	113	.................Hudson.................	5 37p
12 50p	141	Ar ⎰ **ALBANY-RENSSELAER**.......⎰ Dp	5 10p
1 05p	141	Dp ⎱ ⎱ Ar	4 45p
e 1 23p	148	.........Watervliet ⊕ (D&H Sta./gare D&H).........	e 4 05p
e 1 41p	162	.............Mechanicville⊕.............	e 3 43p
2 14p	186	.............Saratoga Springs.............	3 05p
2 39p	204	.........Fort Edward (*Glens Falls and Lake George*)......	2 40p
3 08p	226	Ar ⎰.........Whitehall⊕ (*Rutland*).........⎰ Dp	2 16p
3 13p	226	Dp ⎱ ⎱ Ar	2 12p
e 3 45p	248	.........Fort Ticonderoga⊕.................	e 1 42p
e 4 30p	277	.................Westport⊕................. (*Elizabethtown, Lake Placid, and Saranac Lake*)	e 1 00p
5 32p	316	.................Plattsburgh.................	12 00n
6 00p	340	Ar ⎰.........Rouses Point, NY⊕.........⎰ Dp	11 32a
6 05p	340	Dp ⎱ (U.S. Customs/douane E.-U.) ⎱ Ar	11 22a
|	346	.... Lacolle, PQ (Canada Customs/douane Canada)....	|
d 7 34p	377	.................Montreal West.................	r10 27a
7 45p	382	Ar.............**MONTREAL, PQ**.............Dp (Windsor Station/gare Windsor)	10 15a

A trainman named Thomas W. Jackson, hearing tales like these spun in the smoking car, began to jot them down. Later he put them into a joke book titled *On a Slow Train Through Arkansas*, which was about as corny a collection of jokes as anybody ever assembled. But bored passengers bought copies from the train butchers in such numbers that Jackson soon became rich. More than seven million copies of the book were sold, making it one of the greatest best sellers of all time. Once in a while a copy turns up. If you happen to see one, prepare yourself for such puns as, "You are not the only pebble on the beach, for there is a little rock in Arkansas."

The Erie Railroad was the victim of many slow train jokes, especially concerning its commuter service. Officials of the line thought it would be entertaining for the railroad to join the fun instead of being the victim, so they published jokes about the railroad in the Erie timetables. Whenever a new timetable was published, a fresh set of jokes collected from passengers appeared in print. The officials figured that in this way the passengers soon would get tired of their fun and quit. That's the way it worked out, too.

In truth, many of the jokes the passengers told about the Erie weren't very funny, a fact that became apparent when they were put down on paper. Here are two examples:

A Sad Case

"This is a sad case," said the attendant at an insane asylum, pausing before a padded cell. "There is no hope for the patient whatever."

"What's the trouble?" asked the visitor.

"He thinks he understands an Erie timetable."

Half Fare

A patriarch, who presented a half ticket for a ride between Suffern and Jersey City, was informed that he must pay full fare. He replied, "When I purchased that ticket before boarding the train I was entitled to the half-fare rate."

No wonder that after a couple of years the passengers told the railroad, "Enough! We'll quit the jokes if you will."

Among the railroad yarns spun in the smoking cars were some true ones, such as how the Santa Fe Railroad once prevented a flood from stopping a wedding. In the little community of Rocky Ford, Colorado, in the late 1880's, the station agent, Lee Charles Gillan, was to marry Ida Wickham, daughter of the boarding-house keeper. Since Rocky Ford had no minister, the couple engaged a minister from Las Animas to come over by train and perform the ceremony. The minister's train was due at 11:00 A.M. But a flood had washed out a railroad bridge and the train was stalled on the other side, at La Junta.

The Rocky Ford railroad telegrapher came to the rescue. Tap-

Old print shows railroad in Animas Canyon, Colorado.

ping out dots and dashes, he asked the stranded minister through the telegrapher at La Junta to check with a lawyer and find out whether a wedding by telegraph would be legal. Back came word from the La Junta lawyer that it would be. So the marriage was performed by wire. The minister in La Junta asked, "Do you, Lee, take this woman to be your lawfully wedded wife?" The telegrapher sent the message on the telegraph to Rocky Ford.

Back came the cluster of dots and dashes which, deciphered, said, "I do."

The same question and answer clicked out for Ida. Then came the telegraphed pronouncement, "I hereby pronounce you man and wife."

Everyone pitched into Mother Gillan's platters of fried chicken —except the minister, of course, who sat miles away on the other side of the washed-out bridge and wished he were on hand for his serving.

Then there is the story of the traveling baby who lost his father. This happened on the Santa Fe, too. When the eastbound California Limited stopped at Kansas City one night, a father, who was going to Michigan accompanied by his ten-month-old infant son in a carrying basket, left the train to purchase a package of cigarettes. By the time he returned to the platform, the train had gone, baby and all.

The father was frantic. When they discovered the unaccompanied baby aboard, the Limited's trainmen felt almost as uneasy. Once more the railroad telegraph came to the rescue. The Limited was flagged to an unscheduled stop at Henrietta, Missouri. There the conductor picked up a copy of the infant's feeding formula, which had been forwarded by wire from the anxious father stranded at the Kansas City station.

In the kitchen of the dining car, the conductor mixed the formula as instructed. He gave the baby his bottle at 3:00 A.M. and 6:00 A.M. A Pullman porter was assigned to stand by all night for diaper changes. Word of the plight flashed ahead by telegraph, and when the train pulled into the Dearborn Street Station in Chicago, a crowd of hundreds was on hand to meet it, including a police squad and reporters.

116

The Santa Fe Limited

The father followed on the next available train. When he sought to claim his son, the police at first didn't believe that he really was the father, not a possible kidnapper. He finally satisfied them that he was indeed the father—and also the owner of $5,000 worth of bonds that had been left on the train beside the baby's basket.

And finally, there is the true tale about how Santa Claus drove a locomotive instead of his team of reindeer. For many years an engineer named Joe Gerard had piloted a train on a local run through northern Texas and southern Oklahoma. The area was poorly developed. The residents along the track included poor settlers scrambling to make a living, using log cabins and shacks for homes. Friendly Engineer Joe felt sorry for them and developed the habit of tossing bits of needed provisions from the locomotive cab as the train puffed past these ramshackle homes. Naturally this made him a popular and well known figure. When news reached him of a baby born along the route, he delivered gifts of diapers, blankets, and other necessities to the new mother.

Eventually Joe had the idea of dressing up like Santa Claus on one trip each Christmas season. He loaded the locomotive cab with candy and other gifts—some paid for out of his own pocket, others by donations from persons who learned of his trip. On the

117

appointed day, children gathered near the track over the entire route. Along came the train, with Santa Claus in his red suit and white beard (slightly tinged with cinders) seated high in the locomotive cab, one hand on the throttle and the other tossing gifts from his load into the expectant crowd below.

The sleek big-name express trains racing to meet their schedules didn't have time for such kindly behavior. That's what made the slow country trains such fun at times, even if their passengers often were bored almost to death by the long time it took to steam from one town to the next.

9

TRAIN ROBBERIES

A Rock Island passenger train with a mail car up front rolled west through the cornfields of Iowa on a run from the state capital, Des Moines, to Council Bluffs on the east bank of the Missouri River on a hot midsummer night about a hundred years ago. The locomotive headlight illuminated parallel rails of iron reaching into the darkness ahead. Everything was routine, both in Engineer Rafferty's cab and in the passenger coaches behind.

As the locomotive bent around a curve near Adair, Iowa, Rafferty's fireman shouted, "Look at the track!"

The two men were amazed to see a rope fastened to a piece of track suddenly grow taut. It tugged the rail out of position, creating a gap in the locomotive's path. The engineer jammed his vehicle into reverse, but not in time. The train hit the open track and toppled over on its side with a hiss of steam, crushing the engineer to death. The fireman jumped free.

A gang of men—about a half dozen, by the testimony of the astounded and frightened passengers and crew—leaped from the underbrush at the side of the railroad right-of-way. Two ran directly to the express car, pulled themselves up through its side door, waved the express messenger into submission with their guns, and ordered him to unlock the safe. They scooped up everything it contained.

Others climbed aboard the passenger coaches. "Throw your

money in here!" one ordered, extending the mouth of a grain sack. "All of it!"

Some passengers complied immediately. Others hesitated, until the barrel of a gun was thrust under their noses. Then they obeyed quickly enough.

"Your watches, too!" the leader snapped. "We want everything. Right now."

The robbers worked their way through the entire train, taking everything they could put into their sack. Joining the men who had rifled the express safe, they disappeared into the darkness to the spot where they had hidden their horses—a clean getaway.

This wasn't the first train robbery, for such holdups had been happening on American railroads for several years, but it was notable because it was the first time the notorious Jesse James and his gang, including the ruffian Younger brothers, had tried their hand at terrorizing trains. Previously they had concentrated on robbing small-town banks and stage coaches. Robbing trains was more exciting, and the chances of making a large haul of cash seemed much greater.

Actually, the James and Younger gangsters collected only about $4,000 in their first train holdup, a small "take" compared to the loot collected in some other train robberies. But it was so easy that they took up this form of crime steadily.

Hundreds of trains were robbed during the last three decades of the 1800's and early in the 1900's. Heavy amounts of cash and negotiable valuables were carried aboard trains in those days, locked in safes on the express cars. These cars were wooden and fairly easy to break into. If a stubborn messenger in one of them risked his life by shooting at the robbers rather than opening the door of the car at their command, a stick of dynamite under the car blasted it open, often killing the messenger. The locomotives of the period were light enough that wooden ties piled on the track could stop or derail them. Train robbery became a common form of crime, especially in the West where distances between stations were long and it was relatively easy for gangs of robbers to find remote places at which to waylay the trains.

Outlaw gangs flourished, made up of rough, vicious men who

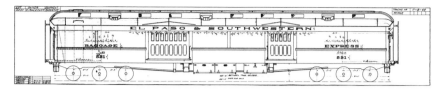

Baggage and express car in the planning stage

didn't hesitate to kill anyone who got in their way. The gangs usually hid out at remote farms, planning their robberies, then rode horseback to the sites selected for their crimes and hid their horses in groves of trees or underbrush.

The doubtful distinction of committing the first American train robbery usually is awarded to the Reno gang of southern Indiana, four tough brothers named Reno and their accomplices. Somehow nobody had thought of robbing a train until the Renos did so just after the Civil War, in 1866. A passenger train on the Ohio & Mississippi Railway had pulled out of Seymour, Indiana, about dusk when two men who had appeared to be ordinary travelers stepped from the front passenger car into the express car ahead. The rear doors of express cars weren't kept locked in those days because nobody expected an attack.

Old print shows robbery of a Union Pacific express car.

Pointing a gun at the express messenger, the two men took his keys, opened the safe, and found $13,000 in it. One pulled the bell cord running through the cars to the locomotive. Heeding the signal, which he believed had been given by the conductor, the unsuspecting engineer stopped the train. This made it easy for the robbers to push another safe out the express car's side door, jump lightly to the ground, and disappear into the darkness.

Startled by such an unheard-of-attack, the trainmen gathered by the locomotive. "What should we do now?" one asked.

"Guess we'd better take the train to the next station and tell them what happened," another replied, which is what they did.

At the station, a search party was organized. It pumped back to the scene of the robbery on a handcar and found the safe at the side of the track, unopened. The robbers hadn't been able to get into it, but they had ridden away $13,000 richer for a few minutes' effort. News of the robbery spread along the telegraph and by word of mouth. Soon more such stickups occurred in several states: Iowa, Missouri, Kansas, and California.

The arch foes of train robbers were the Pinkertons, detectives working for the Pinkerton agency. Their efforts to outwit and outshoot the train-robber gangs resembled those of the Federal Bureau of Investigation agents against John Dillinger and other gangs of bank robbers in the Depression years of the 1930's, half a century later.

A common way for robbers to stop a passenger train was for two of them to slip aboard it at a station and hide between the front of the express car and the rear of the locomotive tender. When the train had steamed out into the country, the men crawled up over the coal pile in the tender, jumped down into the engineer's cab with drawn guns, subdued the engineer and the fireman as the train sped on, and ordered them to stop it at a designated place. There the outlaws were joined by confederates who were hiding near the tracks. Occasionally they would order a trainman to disconnect the express car from the passenger coaches and have the engine pull it ahead to an isolated spot. Thus they were safe from attack by anyone coming from the passenger cars while they broke into the express car.

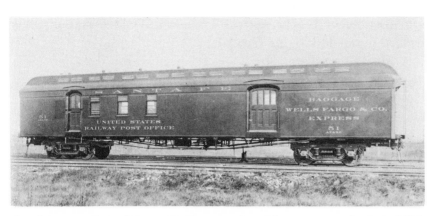

Combination United States Railway mail and baggage car, built in 1902

Modern railway express baggage cars are more secure than the old wooden coaches.

Few of the gangs escaped justice or death in the long run. The Pinkertons were clever, persistent private detectives who came to know the operating methods of most train robbers and tracked down many of them, sometimes long after the holdup had taken place. Shootouts blazed during some robberies, especially when an express car messenger was tough and well armed, as most of them came to be.

One of the fiercest robberies of that raucous era took place at Winston, Missouri, against a Rock Island train, the next-to-last such attack the Jesse James gang ever made. The date was July 15, 1881. Jesse and Frank James and three other gang members, traveling separately to avoid creating suspicion, rode their horses into a stand of timber not far from the Winston station, then walked in the dark to the station.

A short time later the evening train stopped. The James brothers and one accomplice climbed aboard the coaches as if they were passengers. The other two men hid behind the coal tender. Their assignment was to subdue the engineer and fireman, take control of the locomotive, and either move it or keep it stopped, according to orders they received from Jesse. After the train left Winston, the two climbed forward over the coal tender, fired their guns into the air, and yelled to frighten the engine crew. As the engineer stopped the train, the robbers in the locomotive heard shots being fired back in the smoking car.

In that car, Conductor William Westfall was collecting tickets from those who had boarded at Winston. A bearded man in a long linen duster, a loose garment that covered his other clothing, jumped up from a seat, drew his gun, and ordered Westfall to raise his hands.

Bravely, or foolishly, the conductor reached for his own gun, instead.

"Draw that gun and I'll kill you!" the outlaw snarled.

The conductor put his hand down for the gun instead of up above his head. The gunman fired, killing the conductor. Another of the three bandits opened fire, too, and a stonemason named Frank McMillan, a passenger, fell fatally wounded.

Jesse ran forward and entered the express car through its rear door. Frank and an accomplice climbed to the ground and hastened to the side door of the express car. They found the express messenger standing in the open door, trying to see what was happening. Frank grabbed him by a leg and yanked him from the car to the ground.

"Get this train moving!" Jesse shouted to the men holding the locomotive. They pointed their guns close to the engineer and told him to start. He pretended he couldn't, that the brakes were frozen. One robber seized a piece of coal and struck him on the head.

"Get going or I'll kill you!"

That was enough for the engineer. Instead of starting the train slowly, as he normally would do, he threw the throttle wide open. The train jumped ahead with a jerk. The engineer and fireman, terrified, climbed out of their cab onto the outer walkway of the moving locomotive. They were only a few feet from the robbers but had the protection of darkness. The gangsters fired into the dark, more to scare the trainmen than to hit them. Frank James scrambled from the express car over the tender into the cab and pulled back the throttle to slow the train. The robbers jumped from the still-moving locomotive into the blackness. Moments later Jesse James leaped from the side door of the express car with the loot.

From there, the robbers walked to their hidden horses and rode into a pasture, where they divided the booty. It amounted to less than $800. For that, two men had been ruthlessly shot to death.

After this, the James gang robbed only one more train; they collected enough cash from the express car, and watches and cash from the passengers, to give each participant only $140. Train robbing wasn't always a sure way to get rich. Then they went into hiding.

Jesse had somehow become a kind of national hero, foolishly lionized by people who admired his daring and ignored the fact that he violated the law and murdered people in cold blood. A Robin Hood story was circulated about Jesse, claiming that he robbed the rich to aid the poor. It wasn't true.

He disappeared from public view, living in St. Joseph, Missouri, with his wife and two children under the assumed name of Thomas Howard. A heavy reward for his capture had been posted. Two recent recruits in his gang, brothers Robert and Charles Ford, stayed as guests in the James home for a few days. After breakfast on April 3, 1882, the three men went into the living room. Jesse laid his guns on a bed. Then, like any husband helping his wife do household chores, he stepped up on a chair to straighten and dust a picture.

Catching James unarmed and unaware, with his back turned, Bob Ford pulled out a pistol and shot him dead. Instead of being praised for eliminating a notorious outlaw, Ford was condemned by many for betraying a friend. A popular ballad that portrayed

Stagecoach and train robberies occurred by the hundreds in the Old West. Here passengers switch from a train to waiting stagecoaches.

Jesse as a well-intentioned fellow included these lines:

> But that dirty little coward
> That shot Mr. Howard
> Had laid poor Jesse in his grave.

That was the end of the James train-robbing band, in any case. Frank James lost heart after Jesse was killed. He surrendered, turned law-abiding, and lived peacefully for many more years.

Spectacular train robberies occurred often in the West. Rich stores of gold and silver from the California and Nevada mines were shipped East in the express cars, providing robbers with alluring targets. Despite efforts at secrecy, word sometimes slipped out when a special shipment of bullion was to be made. Other targets were the large payrolls dispatched from San Francisco to the mining camps.

The man who arranged one of the first of these robberies was a Sunday School superintendent in Reno, Nevada, known in the community for the kindly way in which he taught children the Ten Commandments. His name was John Chapman and the time was 1870, a boom period in the mines along the Comstock Lode at Virginia City, a short distance south of Reno.

Ignoring his own lessons that "Thou shalt not steal," Chapman organized a gang of six other Reno men whose intention was to rob a train coming across the Sierra Nevadas to Nevada from San Francisco, carrying Wells Fargo express boxes loaded with gold coins for the payrolls.

Chapman, as head of the gang, gave himself a job that would keep him away from the peril of the actual holdup. He went from Reno to San Francisco to find when a heavy consignment of payroll coin would be dispatched. The gang had a code arranged by which Chapman could send word. One day a telegram from San Francisco was delivered to a gang member, R.A. Jones, in Reno: "Send me 60 and charge to the account of J. Enrique." This appeared to be an ordinary business telegram. When decoded, it said that the gold shipment was aboard Central Pacific train No. 1, which had left San Francisco that day. It also tipped the gang that they must deal with six men in sacking the express car.

At 2:00 A.M. the train stopped at Verdi, a small station a few miles west of Reno, and loaded a small amount of freight in the baggage car. The conductor waved his lantern in the "All aboard" signal to the engineer, noticing as he did so that three men were climbing onto the front platform of the baggage car. Assuming that they were hobos, he hurried forward through the passenger coaches to throw them off before the train gathered too much momentum.

As he stepped onto the platform of the front passenger coach, he encounted the masked men with drawn pistols. Startled, he stepped back into the coach and pulled the bell cord for the engineer to stop the train. It was no use. The gang had cut the cord. Soon the train stopped, anyway. Other gang members had crawled forward over the stacks of small logs in the wood-burning locomotive's tender and ordered the engineer to halt.

"We're cutting the express car off from the rest of the train," he was told at gunpoint. "When we tell you to start going, do it!"

The engineer did as he was told. He pulled the express car forward, separating it from the rest of the train, until the locomotive and the single car reached a quarry which the gang used as headquarters.

Along with the express messenger, the engineer and fireman were locked into the mail compartment at one end of the express car. The outlaws piled wooden ties across the track a considerable distance behind, to prevent the unattached passenger coaches from rolling too far down the grade into the middle of their robbery.

From their impromptu jail, the three trainmen heard the robbers hammering open the boxes of gold on the other side of the door. After a few minutes one gunman released them, and from the side door they saw the outlaws on the ground beside the track, running their hands through the mass of gold coins and pouring them into sacks. The bandits were last seen hauling the sacks into the darkness of the quarry. Moments later, the sound of horses' hoofs was heard. The robbers had escaped, carrying with them $41,000 in gold.

They didn't keep the money long, however. Wells Fargo detectives from California were rushed to Reno. Placing close watch on the little desert city's gambling halls, they learned that a local man was tossing money around recklessly—far more money than he normally had. They detained him, questioned him relentlessly, broke down his story that he had been on a lucky gambling streak, and forced him to confess.

Not only did he tell his own role in the robbery but he supplied the names of his partners.

Having managed neatly to stay out of the robbery itself, Chapman, its organizer, returned to Reno from San Francisco. Descending from the train at the Reno station, he was shocked to have detectives step forward and arrest him. When brought to court, two of the seven men turned state's evidence against their partners to save themselves. Less than two months after the holdup, five of the men including Chapman were sent to the state prison for terms averaging twenty years. They paid a high price for their few days of enjoying the illicit pleasure of dipping their hands into the cascade of gold coins. Most of the loot was recovered, except the thousands of dollars some of the men had lost in gambling.

Occasionally a man attempted a train robbery single-handed,

*The men who ran the trains, such as this crew ready to take their loco-
motive on a fast run in 1906, were brave. They never knew when
train robbers would strike on the long, lonely expanses of track.*

an enormously risky procedure but lucrative if successful, since
he had all the loot for himself. One such holdup resulted in a
weird chase sequence that might have come out of an early day
movie.

A little man wearing gold-rimmed glasses and a derby, and
carrying a small suitcase, climbed aboard the front platform of an
express car on a New York Central train at Syracuse, New York,
one bitter February day in 1892. Nobody saw him get aboard.
Once the train was rolling, he strapped his derby hat and case to
the car platform railing, put on a mask, pulled himself onto the
roof, and hung a rope ladder over the side. The rope was fastened
to the car roof.

Oliver C. Perry, for such was his name, climbed down the rope and hung precariously from the side of the train as it rolled along at forty miles an hour. His purpose was to peek through the glass on the side door of the express car to watch the movements of the armed messenger inside. It was a foolhardy stunt. His hands were so cold he barely could hang on. Dangling from the rope as it swung in space, he almost was knocked off by the side of a bridge. But he was able to observe the guard undetected.

When the guard relaxed at one end of the car, Perry pulled open the door and swung himself inside, gun in hand. The amazed messenger reacted instantly, reaching for his gun. Perry fired first, wounding the guard. As Perry seized some valuable-looking packages, the guard pulled the bell cord to stop the train. This alerted the conductor. He climbed onto the rail of the express car's rear platform and looked through the bell-cord hole. Seeing a masked man, he set the handbrakes. This caused Perry to open fire and order the conductor to give the engineer a go-ahead signal. The train rolled on to the next town, where men rushed the express car. Inside, they found the wounded messenger but no robber. Perry apparently was hiding on the roof.

Resuming its trip, the train reached the town of Lyons. There, by chance, a trainman noticed a small man in gold-rimmed glasses with a small case strapped over one shoulder. He recalled having seen the same man back at the Syracuse station.

"How did he get here so quickly?" the trainman wondered.

He stepped forward to question the man. Frightened, Perry—that's who it was—pulled a gun and ran to a freight train nearby. He waved the crew away, uncoupled the locomotive, and, shoving the throttle open, fled down the track aboard it.

Two trainmen armed with shotguns gave chase in a passenger locomotive. At that point the New York Central had four tracks, and the two locomotives were on adjoining tracks. The pursuers in the faster passenger locomotive were catching up with Perry. Realizing this, he jammed on his engine's brakes and fired into the other locomotive as it sped past. They slowed down and returned the fire. He sped up again.

Down the tracks they went, shooting it out, until Perry's locomotive ran low on steam. He stopped it, jumped to the ground with his valise, and disappeared into the underbrush.

For all his brash daring, Perry didn't get away with it. A sheriff's posse eventually caught him, and he was sentenced to forty-nine years in prison.

Train robbery continued with some frequency well into the 1900's, then diminished. No train has been held up for many years. Steel express cars are far more secure than the old wooden ones. Communications between trains and the ground are fast now, by radio. Train robbers were successful mostly because they stopped the trains in remote places where no warning could be given easily. Today, with swift electronic communications and signal systems that show where trains are situated at all times, such isolation is impossible. Helicopters and planes could be summoned instantly to search the area, in case a gang were to attempt such a crime. Nor are large shipments of cash made by train any longer.

Train robbery, a daring and slightly romantic but frequently vicious practice, has become an almost forgotten form of crime.

10

WRECKS AND RESCUES

His name was John Luther Jones, but everyone called him Casey . . . Casey Jones, the most famous locomotive engineer in history. He died at the throttle of the speeding Chicago to New Orleans express train of the Illinois Central Railroad, popularly called the Cannonball, the night of April 29, 1900, and was immortalized in a catchy song about his deeds on that fatal misty night in western Tennessee.

Thousands of persons, trainmen and passengers, have been killed in train wrecks on American railroads, especially in the years around the turn of the century. Passenger trains were running faster and faster, but railroads were not protected by the automatic block signals and other safety devices in use today. Many lines had only single tracks, requiring one train to pull onto a siding while another passed it on the main line.

This was arranged by orders handed to the engineer at each station, based on information telegraphed along the wire that paralleled the track. If the dot-dash messages were garbled, or an engineer failed to understand or obey the rules and orders, smashups occurred. Since the coaches of the trains were made of wood well into the twentieth century, they collapsed and splintered easily in a collision, frequently resulting in horrible wrecks and high casualties.

Casey was an engineer whose pride was getting his train to its

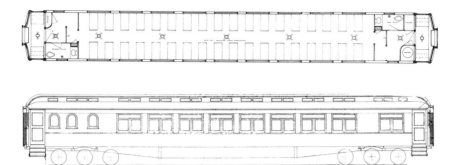

The old cars made of wood gave little protection to passengers in a wreck. A wooden 68-seat coach built for the 1904 Exhibit in St. Louis, and a 16-section wooden sleeper, 1905.

destination on time. That meant riding with the throttle wide open and occasionally bending the rules a bit.

His assignment that night was to haul the southbound Cannonball from Memphis to Canton, Mississippi, a distance of 188 miles, through blackness and low murky skies. Riding with him as fireman was Sim Webb, whose job was to shovel coal into the hungry maw of Casey's favorite locomotive, No. 382, and "keep her hot." The train arrived at Memphis very late from Chicago; by the time Casey and Sim pulled the six cars out of the Poplar Street Station in Memphis the train was ninety-five minutes behind schedule, a performance so bad that it was embarrassing to the Illinois Central, which boasted about its on-time trips.

Casey's orders were, "Make up that time. Get her into Canton on schedule."

Ninety-five minutes to make up in 188 miles! That meant running a minute faster than regular schedule every two miles of his run.

As the famous ballad told the story after his death:

> Casey Jones—mounted to his cabin—
>   Casey Jones—with his orders in his hand—
> Casey Jones—mounted to his cabin,
>   Took a farewell trip to the Promised Land.

From Memphis to Granada the single track of the Illinois Cen-

Casey Jones

tral was level and fairly straight. Casey's orders included no meetings with other trains or station stops. He could let 'er roll, and did. With wide open throttle, No. 382's headlight marking two straight lines of steel ahead, the Cannonball hurtled along. By the time Casey applied the brakes and pulled into the Granada station for a five-minute stop, he had made up sixty of the ninety-five minutes. Eighty-eight miles of track lay ahead to Canton, the end of his run. At Winona, twenty-three miles south of Granada, Casey's watch showed the train only fifteen minutes late.

Onward the Cannonball sped. Sim kept the steam high by shoveling in the coal, scoop after scoop. As the train passed stations and switches, Casey pulled the cord on his special whistle, an instrument of six thin tubes fastened together through which steam was forced like a small circus calliope. Casey's delicate touch produced such distinctive sounds that persons hearing the train whistle knew he was at the throttle.

The switchmen knew by the engine's moans
That the man at the throttle was Casey Jones.

When the express train neared the little town of Vaughan, four-teen miles north of Casey's destination at Canton, obstacles developed. The northbound train to Chicago pulled onto a siding to let Casey pass. But he faced a slowdown at Vaughan. Two freight trains headed in opposite directions were ordered to pull off onto a side passing track, three-fifths of a mile long, at the Vaughan station while the Cannonball passed. When both were on the siding, they more than filled it, so that a few cars from one train or the other had to stick out onto the main track.

Casey was under instructions to "saw" through them. That is, the orders were for the overflow onto the main track to be at the southern, or far, switch. After Casey drove his train clear of the north switch, the freight trains were to advance to the north so the southern switch would be clear. Thus the overflow would move into the main line behind the rear of the express. "Sawing" is a common maneuver on single track railroads.

Since no electric signals existed on this section of the Illinois Central then, the maneuver had to be done by hand lantern signals. It would have been simple enough, except that unbeknown to the onrushing Casey, an air hose had broken on one of the freights, so that it could not "saw" south as ordered. That left four cars of one freight sticking out past the northern switch onto the main line.

A brakeman from the freight train, aware that the Cannonball was speeding south toward the switch, ran north up the main line. He placed a torpedo on the track, a warning that would explode when a wheel passed over it. Then he hurried further north, to a point more than a half mile beyond the switch, waving a red lantern.

The Cannonball's headlight bore down on him at seventy miles an hour. Frantically he waved the lantern. To his dismay, Casey didn't slow down a bit. Apparently he thought the swinging light was a warning about the expected obstacle at the southern switch more than a mile away.

Locomotive No. 382, which Casey Jones rode to his death. Casey was not in the engineer's seat when this photograph was taken.

Within seconds the locomotive wheels exploded the torpedo. Casey jammed on the brakes. Around the curve into Vaughan the train rushed. Sim, the fireman, looked out the left side of the locomotive and to his horror saw the taillights of the freight's caboose on the main line just ahead.

"Jump for your life!" he shouted at Casey.

The engineer yelled back, "You jump. I'll stay."

Sim leaped out, rolling to the dirt clear of the train. Casey tried mightily to stop his train, but there wasn't time. His locomotive plowed into the rear of the freight and fell off the track. Casey was still at his post. When his body was found, one hand held the throttle, the other the air-brake control. No one else died in the wreck, just Casey.

Why he violated railroad rules by ignoring the brakeman's lantern never was learned, but the action cost him his life.

Although far worse railroad wrecks have occurred, this one became renowned because an Illinois Central shopworker named Wallace Saunders, who had known and admired Casey Jones, made up a song about it. Its catchy words and melody were picked up by other men, and eventually a professional songwriter dressed it up a bit. Soon millions of copies were sold, and it became one of the country's best-loved folk songs. On the fiftieth anniversary of the wreck, a special United States postage stamp was issued honoring Casey, and through him all locomotive engineers.

Train wrecks have happened from strange causes, unrelated to mistakes by humans or breakdowns in equipment.

There was the time, for example, when the Commercial Traveler of the Clover Leaf Line, rolling across the flat land of central Indiana in 1916, was struck broadside by a tornado and lifted off the track, coming to earth twenty feet off the right-of-way. The passengers were trapped for four hours until help could reach them. In another display of nature's force, a forest fire roaring across Minnesota near Hinckley set the wooden coaches of a passing train ablaze. Most of the passengers fled the train and survived by lying in the mud and water of a nearby lake.

Then there was the wreck witnessed by thirty thousand spectators who paid for the privilege of seeing it happen. This was a stunt to sell tickets, staged by the Katy, as the Missouri, Kansas & Texas Railway is called. The Katy's general passenger agent promised that he could attract twenty thousand people to a remote area of Texas in 1896 to watch two trains collide head-on. He was a clever man, understanding the strange human desire to watch destruction—the same urge that makes demolition derbies of old automobiles at racetracks so popular.

Posters plastered in towns for hundreds of miles advertised the spectacle. The Katy ran seven special trains from Dallas-Fort Worth carrying passengers to the scene at $2.00 a head, and other trains brought thousands more sight-seers. The throng was 50 per cent larger than the optimistic promoter had expected.

Munching refreshments purchased at concession stands the railroad had installed, the huge crowd gathered in late afternoon. Spectators clambered onto every vantage point near the spot marked for the collision. Two locomotives, each with six passenger coaches attached, stood nose to nose. At a signal, they backed

137

in opposite directions up hillsides, like boxers going into their corners after shaking hands, or duelists pacing off the required number of steps before turning and firing. At the starting signal, each engineer opened the throttle of his locomotive, tied down the whistle cord, and jumped to the ground from the rolling engine. The unmanned trains rushed down the slopes, each going sixty miles an hour, whistles screeching. Torpedos placed on the tracks exploded, adding to the racket.

Boom!

The engines smashed into each other and exploded in a cloud of steam. The smokestack of one landed a quarter of a mile away. The wheel trucks from beneath one coach were hurled three hundred yards, despite their weight of a ton. The crowd gasped, then cheered. A farmer fell from a tree and broke his leg. Three spectators were killed by flying debris. The railroad counted its dollars from the tickets and pronounced the wreck a great success.

Along with the stories of train wrecks there are tales of heroism and rescue, in which quick thinking and bravery prevented tragedy. Perhaps the first of these occurred on the Erie Railroad near Oswego, New York, in 1854, when railroading was in its infancy. Mrs. Silas Horton saw a fallen tree across the track near her home. She could hear the mail train whistling in the distance. Mrs. Horton thought quickly. She knew the mail train had to be flagged down and that red was the warning color. So she grabbed a pair of long red underpants—yes, people really wore such

Pullman Standard riveted-frame, six-wheel passenger truck developed for steel cars

things then—and dashed from her home. Waving the underwear wildly, she got the engineer's attention in time for him to halt the train and prevent a wreck. Her reward was a pair of lifetime passes on the Erie for herself and her husband.

The role of national heroine came to Kate Shelley, a fifteen-year-old Iowa farm girl, to her embarrassment, because of the daring manner in which she saved the Chicago and North Western's Midnight Express from disaster in a storm a hundred years ago. Kate's father, a former railroad man, was dead, and she helped her mother run the small family farm along the North Western tracks not far from Boone, Iowa. The year was 1881. In fact, being a sturdy girl, Kate did much of the farming herself. At twilight on July 6, when she went out to the barn in heavy rain to milk the cows, she noticed that Honey Creek at the lower edge of the farm had overflowed. Its waters had backed up alongside the embankment carrying the track to the Honey Creek bridge.

About eleven o'clock, Kate and her mother, sitting by candle-light in their parlor, heard a locomotive whistle. Both knew the schedule by heart. No train was due from either direction.

"See, there's a headlight," Kate exclaimed. A locomotive travel-ing alone, sent out to test the line, rolled out onto the Honey Creek bridge. Suddenly the headlight disappeared. A loud crash and the hiss of escaping steam followed. The Honey Creek bridge had collapsed and the locomotive had tumbled into the stream.

Both women knew what that meant. The bridge was out and the Midnight Express was due to pass there soon. In the thunder-ing, lashing storm, the engineer wouldn't be able to see the gap in the track in time. A tragic train wreck was in the making.

"I'm going over there," Kate told her mother. She lit the rail-road lantern her father had once used, bundled herself into a coat, and headed into the storm.

Floodwaters from the creek had engulfed the Shelley farm, except for the knoll where the house stood and a ridge of land leading to the railroad embankment. Scrambling along the track, Kate fell and bruised her knee. Much worse, the glass globe of her lantern was cracked open and the flame blew out. Kate had no way to signal the train.

139

Half-crawling, half-running over the track through the black night, she lurched along a trestle over swampland until she reached the station at the little community of Moingona nearby.

The station agent was appalled to see a bedraggled young woman with streaming wet hair appear out of the storm.

"What's this?" he said.

Kate panted, "Honey Creek bridge is out. You'd better stop the express."

The agent ran up the track. When the train appeared a few minutes later, he stopped it with wide-swinging arcs of his red lantern. The passengers swarmed onto the platform and, hearing what Kate had done, engulfed her with thanks and congratulations. Soon she was a national heroine. Collections were taken up in her honor, and she was given a scholarship to Simpson College.

Kate went to college for a year but didn't like it. She taught school for a while (it didn't take much education to be a country schoolteacher then), but wanted to be back on the farm. The grateful North Western appointed her its agent at Moingona; there she spent the remaining years of her life in charge of the station where her act of heroism had occurred. Years later when a lofty steel bridge was built to replace the trestle, it was named the Kate Shelley Bridge, a lasting memorial to a brave teenage girl whose deed has been almost forgotten.

Another moment of quick thinking in a storm—this time a snowstorm—saved the passengers aboard an East Coast passenger train from being caught in a wreck on Christmas Eve in 1919.

The Philadelphia and Reading Railroad's Express No. 620 steamed out of Philadelphia in the gloomy dusk, carrying about 150 passengers to New York in time for the holiday. Heavy, driving snow, obscuring the track, almost blotted out the train's headlight as the express neared the long trestle across Newark Bay.

Engineer James Hill strained out the locomotive window to see the signal lights along the track, anxious to maintain his schedule despite the storm. Without warning, an object flying through the snow struck the engineer in the right eye and on the forehead. He was stunned, knocked from his seat, and fell unconscious to the floor of the locomotive cab.

As a young girl in 1881, Kate Shelley saved a passenger train from disaster in a storm at Moingona, Iowa. She stands at the station, where she later was named agent as a reward for her heroism. (Note the old Chicago and North Western baggage hand truck at left.)

Hill's guiding hand was pulled from the throttle as he fell. The train rolled on, uncontrolled, at forty miles an hour toward the trestle. This was before locomotives had the dead man's throttle, a device that cuts off the power whenever the engineer's hand leaves the control. The locomotive on the express was of a type known to trainmen as a Mother Hubbard. The engineer's cab was in the middle and the fireman was stationed twenty feet away at the rear of the boiler, where he couldn't see the engineer.

At his post, Fireman Sam Wood glanced up as the train rolled past a red signal light. Something was wrong! There was danger of some kind ahead, but the train hadn't slowed down. Jim Hill was too good an engineer to do a thing like that.

Sam dropped his shovel, ran around the end of the boiler, and saw Hill sprawled on the floor. He grabbed the emergency brake lever. For a moment the train rushed on, then slowed. Finally it jerked to a stop. Just four hundred feet ahead of it, almost concealed by the falling snow, was another train standing on the trestle! Back in the passenger coaches, the travelers wondered why their train had stopped so suddenly but nobody told them the reason. They went on to their Christmas in New York unaware of how their lives had been saved by an alert fireman. It never was determined what object had struck the engineer, but railroad men suspected that it was a bird buffeted in the snowstorm by the wind.

Railroads have found snowstorms to be among their worst natural enemies. Snows drifted high by blizzard winds in the unprotected open spaces of the West and piled up in mountain passes have caused trains to stall for days. Their passengers were forced to endure hardships while plows struggled to chop their way through the tightly packed white barricades.

Once the snow is cleared from the runway of an airport, an airliner can shake itself free from the earth and soar above snowbound areas to the safe haven of another airport. Railroads are not that fortunate. When snow engulfs the tracks, it may cover the route for many miles, building up to excessive depths in the cuts made through the hills for the railroad bed. That usually is

Passengers from transcontinental train snowbound in New Mexico in 1903 walk in snowbanks piled up beside their stalled coaches. Below: Waiting patiently for the train to move on.

where trains stall, their power subdued by the stubborn, moisture-laden white barriers.

Once a railroad's operations are thrown out of kilter by snow, and its schedules upset, troubles pile up rapidly. A party of vacationers who started from Chicago to Los Angeles aboard a Pullman car on the Chicago, Rock Island & Pacific in 1903, for example, finally arrived in the California city after a trip lasting eight nights and eight-and-a-half days. The scheduled time for the trip was three nights and two days. Their train was snowbound in Kansas, New Mexico, Oklahoma, and Texas. Struggling across western Texas, the train stuck fast in a sixteen-foot snowdrift on the prairie and stayed there for three days. Two more express trains lined up behind it, until six hundred travelers were stranded. The coal-fired locomotives of two trains went dead, leaving the passengers without heat. Those on the first train were luckier. Their engineer managed to keep steam up. When the water supply for his locomotive ran low, male passengers shoveled snow from the drifts outside their cars to fill the tank. A rotary plow pushed by a locomotive attacked the snow barrier from the other side, its blades hurling a screen of white to both sides of the track. When the plow was only twenty feet from the cowcatcher of the first stalled train, it broke down and had to be hauled away.

Some passengers had musical instruments. They played while others sang and danced, trying to keep up a party atmosphere.

Old print shows snowplow struggling to keep the transcontinental track open through the California mountains.

A transcontinental train was stuck in the snow for thirty-eight hours at the tiny community of Leoncito, New Mexico, in 1903, at an altitude of 5,400 feet. Passengers waited at the station for something to happen.

The novelty wore off soon, and the wait turned into an endurance contest.

Soon the food supplies on the trains were exhausted. Children, women, and many of the men passengers and trainmen grew faint with hunger. Two trainmen plodded along the track four miles through the snow to a small country station, where they obtained a few biscuits and other bits of food for the passengers. Despite their strenuous eight-mile round trip, the food they brought back provided nourishment for only a few of the most needy travelers.

Trainmen and passengers working in shifts attacked the remaining twenty-foot barricade with shovels. After they dug a dent in the drift, the locomotive bucked into the snow and cut it down a bit more. Back to the shovels. Another charge by the locomotive. Eventually the path was opened and the three trains reached El Paso—a trip none of their passengers would ever forget.

A far grimmer story of trains stalled in blizzards took place a few years later on the Great Northern Railroad in the state of

Washington. In the spring of 1910, weeks of storms had piled snow thirty feet deep on the Cascade Mountains. A warm spell followed, and numerous small snowslides blocked the tracks until rotary plows could sweep them clear. On February 22, two passenger trains left Spokane for the trip to Seattle. Three days later, repeatedly delayed by slides, they still were stalled at the little town of Leavenworth. By the night of February 27, five days on their way, they steamed through the Cascade Tunnel and drew to a halt on a ledge high above a canyon near the Wellington station. Again their progress was stopped by slides. The trains stood side by side on adjoining tracks.

The skies opened up again on the night of March 1, this time with rain and lightning. The rain draining under the piled-up snow on the mountainside above the tracks caused the drifts to work loose. Without warning, an avalanche rumbled down the slope from a point a thousand feet above the tracks. Smashing everything in its path, it roared across the tracks in a tumultuous white cloud and swept both trains over the ledge into the bottom of the canyon two hundred feet below.

In the tangled debris of shattered coaches and locomotives, 101 passengers and trainmen died that night, never knowing what had hit them.

11

THE STREAMLINERS ARRIVE

A silver streak hurtled down the track out of the west, its approach signaled by the piercing screech of its electric horn. Watchers along the Burlington Railroad tracks on a spring day in 1934 were awed by the roar as it shot past, shaking the ground and stirring a cloud of dust. It vanished toward Chicago. This was the Zephyr, which brought a revolution to American railroading.

The Burlington Zephyr was the first diesel-powered streamliner in the United States made of stainless steel. On that day in May, the new-type passenger train was making an historic dawn-to-dusk dash against the sun a thousand miles from Denver to Chicago to celebrate the opening of that city's second world fair, the Century of Progress.

With seventy-two passengers aboard, the Zephyr flashed across the plains of Nebraska, past the young cornfields of Iowa, and through the flat Illinois prairie dotted with farmhouses without a stop. Speeding through the suburbs of Chicago in the twilight, it snapped a wire stretched across the Burlington track near downtown Chicago, like a runner breaking the tape at the finish line of a race, then rolled slowly onto the Century of Progress grounds, where admiring crowds cheered it.

Forty-one years earlier, at the Columbian Exposition of 1893 in Chicago, visitors had admired Engine 999 and the gleaming

The Burlington Zephyr speeds through Aurora, Illinois, on its historic nonstop run from Denver to Chicago in 1934.

wooden coaches of the Empire State Express, the country's first high-speed train. This time Chicagoans and their guests saw the train that doomed the era of steam locomotives.

Instead of getting its power from steam created by an intense coal fire, the Zephyr locomotive's wheels were turned with electricity created by generators driven by diesel fuel oil. This sleek, streamlined locomotive did not pour out the familiar column of black smoke, only a wisp of diesel exhaust. Its engineer sat high at the very front of the locomotive, in a compartment reminiscent of an airliner's cockpit, behind a curved shield of stainless steel and glass.

The nation gasped at the news of the Zephyr's run. It reached a maximum speed of 112 miles per hour and averaged 77.5 miles per hour for the long run. Its time from Denver to Chicago was 13 hours and 5 minutes, half the normal time for the run by steam train. Speed was not the Zephyr's only virtue; its endurance was equally important. It ran the 1,015 miles without a stop, an unheard-of achievement. The longest nonstop run for steam locomo-

148

tives was a stretch of 401 miles in England. Steam locomotives devoured coal and water, and stops to replenish the tender's supply of these ingredients were essential.

Everyone sensed that a new era in railroad operations was beginning. Thrilling as the Zephyr was, however, few persons realized that in a relatively few years, the diesel locomotives would drive the steam locomotives out of work. Today the only steam locomotives in operation are a handful used on nostalgic sightseeing trips for tourists.

This pioneer run by the Zephyr was so eye-catching that hardly anyone recognized a significant fact: the Zephyr's highest speed of 112 miles an hour didn't quite equal the Empire State Express record of 112.5 miles per hour set four decades earlier. The Zephyr did sustain high speeds for longer periods, however. Record speed for a United States steam train was 115.2 miles per hour on the Philadelphia and Reading Railroad in 1904.

Although it has long been retired from service, the pioneer Zephyr can be seen today parked outside the Museum of Science and Industry in Chicago, open for inspection by visitors to that fascinating building.

Diesel locomotives quickly became popular with the railroad companies because they are cheaper to operate than steam locomotives, are more powerful, and cleaner. Cinders and grime from the plume of smoke trailing from a steam locomotive are absent from diesel locomotives. Also, the diesels can be kept in almost continuous service. In the days of coal-powered steam engines, the "iron steeds," as some writers insisted on calling them, had to be taken into huge sooty roundhouses for frequent servicing. This increased the cost of operating them.

When railroads observed the cost saving in diesels and their reliability, they switched to them as rapidly as the factories could build them. The country's fast "name" trains became even faster. For example, Santa Fe's famous Chief, which carried many Hollywood film stars from Chicago to Los Angeles, made the run in 55 hours with a steam locomotive. Death Valley Scotty's record run over the route was 44 hours and 54 minutes. When the Santa Fe put diesel locomotives and streamlined cars on the route, call-

The plume of smoke above the old steam engines delivered many a cinder to many a passenger's eye. Here the Santa Fe's California Limited is the first train across the new bridge at Canyon Diablo in 1947. Below: *Diesel engine pulls Santa Fe train.*

ing the train the Super Chief, the schedule was reduced by nearly fifteen-and-a-half hours.

The new streamliners speeding along American rail lines were changed drastically inside, as well as at the front end. The standard Pullman sleeping cars with their pull-down upper berths and heavy green curtains, known to the Pullman porters as "battleships," were replaced by ingenious sleeping cars in which every Pullman passenger had a small private room of his own.

Instead of ordering a lower berth or an upper berth, the single passenger engaged a "roomette." In this completely enclosed room, the bed folds into the wall at one end of the space during the daytime. The passenger has a sofa seat, a large window, ample space for his legs, a closet for his clothes, even a private washstand and toilet. A sliding door when closed cuts off the passenger completely from the corridor. He can stay in his roomette for the entire trip and never see another passenger, if he desires. At bedtime, he doesn't need a porter to prepare his bed. He merely turns a handle and the bed swings down into position from the end wall, already made up. The more elaborate trains like the Super Chief even have a choice of piped-in music available at the turn of a knob. A Pullman car passenger has privacy that is impossible to obtain on an airliner.

Clever as the roomettes are in their compact use of space, those who travel in them discover that they are a little tricky. The bed when lowered fills the entire length of the roomette. When the passenger wishes to lower the bed, he must back out into the corridor through the open door. Or a green curtain can be zipped across the opening if the passenger wishes; this bulges when he steps back into the corridor, inside it. He must undress, hang up his clothing, and use the private washroom facilities before lowering the bed, because once down the bed blocks all the space. If he wishes to use these facilities during the night, the passenger must back out into the corridor again and raise the bed.

Bedrooms and compartments for two to four persons also are found on this type of sleeping car, just as they were on the old style ones.

Not only do the new cars provide privacy, including elimina-

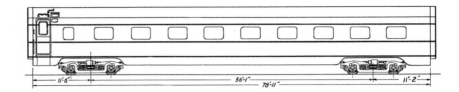

Above: *Roomette car, 1938 design.* Left: *Accommodations with private facilities are available for more than one traveler.* Right: *Washbasin at left folds up into the wall when not in use.*

tion of the old shelf-like upper berths, but they are air conditioned. No longer do passengers have to argue among themselves as to whether they should open a car window to let in fresh air, along with the dirt and cinders. Each roomette and bedroom has individual air-conditioning controls.

In the years just before World War II, the switchover of mainline passenger and freight trains to diesel power moved rapidly. After a pause for the war, when the country concentrated on building tanks and ships instead of luxury trains, more and more diesel locomotives appeared on the rails.

Just as they were completing their switchover to diesels, American railroads ran into trouble. Many passengers stopped riding

A Santa Fe streamliner between Los Angeles and Chicago enters a tunnel in Cajon Pass, California.

Marines arriving at Los Angeles, World War II. Note the old coaches of the troop train at right.

Tank corps members take brief rest beside their troop train.

the trains. Other ways to travel between cities became popular. Faster automobiles were built and highways were paved for them, frequently alongside the railroad tracks. People discovered that they could drive from one town to another about as fast as they could get there on the local passenger train, and could travel whenever they wished. They didn't need to adjust their lives to the train schedule. Bus lines began operating on the highways, for those who didn't have automobiles or didn't care to drive. Soon it was costing the railroads more to operate their local trains than they collected in passenger fares and baggage fees. One by one they canceled these short-haul runs. Long-distance travel by train still was faster and more comfortable than by automobile or bus, however, and the glamorous mainline "name" trains continued to flourish.

During World War II, when gasoline was rationed, train travel had a huge if temporary upsurge. Troop trains reappeared, carrying thousands of American soldiers around the country from training camps to maneuver grounds, and to the embarkation ports on the Atlantic and Pacific coasts, where the men boarded troopships that carried them to battlefields overseas.

Troop trains weren't designed for comfort. Quite the opposite. They didn't need to offer luxuries to attract their passengers in uniform, who were aboard because they were ordered to be there. Often the soldiers were given a railroad's oldest coaches. Many aging veterans of World War II tell unpleasant tales about long, dreadfully slow journeys in troop trains whose coaches were too hot or too cold depending upon the season, always were overcrowded, and often were without enough food aboard to satisfy the soldiers' hunger. American troop trains didn't equal in discomfort the Forty and Eight freight cars that had carried American soldiers in France in World War I—the name meaning that the cars were marked to carry forty men and eight horses—but came close to doing so at times.

Indeed, when some soldiers returned from overseas after World War II, they bought civilian clothes at the ports where they disembarked, then used part of their saved-up army pay to ride

155

Navaho woman weaves a rug as the Santa Fe's El Capitan goes past in northern Arizona. Note the five Diesel units pulling the heavy train and the double-decked passenger cars.

The Southern Pacific's Shasta Daylight twists along the shoreline of Lake Odell, Oregon, in 1951.

home on the luxury trains, just to delight themselves with the comforts of being ordinary citizens again.

During the 1950's, commercial flying became so commonplace and so popular that travelers swarmed to the airliners and abandoned the long-distance trains. Why take a train on an overnight trip between two cities, when you could fly the distance in four or five hours—and, after jetliners came into operation, in two or three? Trains like the Twentieth Century Limited which once ran in several sections because of the demand for tickets made their journeys two-thirds empty. Yet their operating costs remained as high as ever.

One by one, trains whose names had been household words for years were eliminated by the railroads for lack of business. On those that continued to run, service often was poor. The fewer the passengers, the worse the service. This in turn drove away those passengers who resented the rude treatment and the dirty cars with broken equipment.

This writer, wanting to have one last ride on the Twentieth Century Limited, made a trip aboard it to New York in the late 1960's a short time before it was wiped out of existence by the railroad management. The train was a sorry imitation of what the luxurious Century once was. The schedule was slow, the roadbed was rough, the food in the dining car was poor, the upholstery was ragged. The renowned extra touches of Century service were missing; so were most of the passengers. After dinner, in the observation club car which in the old days was so full that passengers had to wait in line for a seat, the writer was the only person present. We pulled into Grand Central Station in New York ninety minutes late. The train was like a ghost of finer days, rattling and creaking.

Although some railroads tried hard to maintain good service under difficult conditions, others made it clear that they would prefer to abandon all their passenger trains and concentrate on the profitable freight business. They were accused with reason of trying to drive passengers away from their trains, and then abandoning the trains because there weren't enough passengers. At times passenger trains had to creep behind freight trains and in

The California Limited on its first run. Later the train became so popular that it was run in several sections. Below: Seven sections of the California Limited prepare to leave Los Angeles.

some instances had to wait on side tracks while freight trains passed. Shades of Casey Jones!

Americans rapidly were losing the railroad travel habit. Millions of boys and girls grew to adulthood without riding on a train—a situation that their grandparents would have had difficulty imagining—or indeed, even seeing a passenger train.

In the northeastern part of the United States particularly, huge railroads that were considered fundamental parts of American business for a hundred years fell into a dangerous financial condition. Instead of making profits, they suffered millions of dollars in losses. Those two traditional giant competitors, the Pennsylvania Railroad and the New York Central Railroad, merged into the Penn Central Railroad. They thought they would wipe out their losses that way. Instead, the losses grew bigger.

One way the struggling railroads tried to save money was to delay, or eliminate, maintenance of their tracks. This led to rotted ties and roadbeds without enough rock ballast to hold the tracks in line. Many trains jumped the track. To reduce the danger of derailments, trains ran under "slow" orders on poor sections of track. Swift diesel locomotives capable of hauling a passenger train easily at ninety miles an hour were forced to creep along at ten or twenty miles an hour, falling far behind schedule. It was not unusual for a supposedly "crack" train to arrive two hours late.

Another corner the railroads cut on their passenger service was failing to replace worn-out cars. Those gleaming streamliner Pullmans and coaches that went into service behind the new diesel locomotives in the 1930's showed their age early in the 1970's. They rattled and squeaked. Their air conditioning didn't work. Seats often were broken.

Altogether, United States passenger train service had fallen into a sorry condition by the start of the 1970's. Some persons predicted that within a few years all passenger trains would disappear except commuter lines near the big cities, a possibility that seemed almost unbelievable in a country which once had twenty thousand trains a day.

159

12

AMTRAK TAKES OVER

The self-closing door of the silvery railroad car slides shut, the train glides slowly away from the station at Washington, D.C., and a conductor calls out, "All tickets, please." The blunt red, white, and blue nose of the four-car train cuts the air with gathering speed, headed for New York City. We are aboard the Metroliner, the fastest train on American rails. Its sleek sides are adorned with a bright symbol and a new word in the American language, Amtrak.

The Metroliner is the most publicized member of the fleet with which the National Railroad Passenger Corporation, operating under the name Amtrak, is trying to rebuild American railroad travel.

Amtrak appeared on the scene in the early 1970's when the federal government heeded the cry "Railroad service must not die!" from those who could see beyond the ragged condition of the surviving trains and understood how important railroads are to America. Congress passed a law setting up a government-controlled railroad passenger corporation. Helped by millions of tax dollars from Congress, the corporation took over control of most passenger trains in the United States.

According to the schedule, the Metroliner should make the 225-mile trip from the national capital to Pennsylvania Station in midtown Manhattan in three hours and one minute—and it does.

Metroliners on the New York-Washington run exceed a hundred miles per hour at one point.

Many but not all of the hourly Metroliners do arrive on time. That is an average speed of seventy-five miles an hour, including hasty stops at five cities along the route to pick up and discharge passengers. Back at the height of steam railroading, the Pennsylvania Railroad bragged that its crack Congressional made the same trip in three hours and thirty-five minutes, thirty-four minutes slower than our schedule.

"Hurry, hurry, hurry!" is the command.

The coach on which we are riding bulges slightly on the sides. Its brightly decorated interior has rounded corners and reclining seats. It resembles an airliner cabin, except that it is more spacious. From a loudspeaker concealed in the ceiling a voice announces, "Ladies and gentlemen, in about two minutes we will arrive in Philadelphia." Moments later, it reports, "We are now arriving at Penn Station, 30th Street, Philadelphia."

Those leaving and entering the train must move quickly. In slightly less than a minute a bell rings, the outer doors close, the train starts, and the doors inside the coaches slide shut again.

The route between Washington and New York is electrified, so Metroliners operate on power drawn from overhead wires rather than being pulled by the diesel locomotives found on most trains in the country today. Metroliners do not have separate locomotives; the engineer sits in a compartment that occupies a small portion of the front coach. On such a short run there are no sleeping cars. The train consists of a parlor car, a snack bar car, and two coaches, one for smokers and one for non-smokers.

Across Pennsylvania and New Jersey the Metroliner speeds, at one point faster than one hundred miles per hour. Its passengers walk from their coaches into the snack car for a light lunch. A quick stop at Newark, and the train noses into the tunnel under the Hudson River.

As the speed slows, the voice announces from the ceiling, "We are now arriving at Penn Station, New York."

The doors slide open, the passengers lift their luggage from overhead racks, and they step out into the terminal on the West Side of Manhattan.

When Amtrak began operation on May 1, 1971, the first thing it did was to eliminate many trains that were still running but were carrying so few passengers that they were doomed, anyway. Amtrak officials selected the most important routes in the country and concentrated their efforts on rebuilding traffic on them. So, on that fateful day, 178 American trains made their last run into oblivion.

Amtrak started life with 182 trains a day connecting about three hundred cities from coast to coast, only a fragment of what American train service had been once, but a foundation for a fresh start. A basic network of passenger service had been saved. Since then, more trains have been added, and more are planned. Now, when we think of going by train, we think Amtrak.

The new system inherited problems so severe that even Amtrak officials didn't realize how much their heads were going to throb. Just painting the Amtrak red, white, and blue pointed-arrow insignia on the sides of the railroad coaches didn't change their dirty, tattered insides. Some coaches Amtrak took over from the railroads were nearly forty years old. Many of the locomotives were badly worn, too, and couldn't perform reliably. Although most of the country's old coaches took on the Amtrak label, a few were converted into such uses as offices and restaurants on wheels.

During the first years of Amtrak's existence, quite a few persons who hadn't ridden a train in years, or ever, were curious enough to try the railroads. Travel by rail jumped way up when the Arab countries cut off oil shipments to the United States in 1974, causing a gasoline shortage. Especially at holiday times, trains that had been almost empty three or four years earlier became jammed. Trying to handle the crowds, Amtrak had to put into service even older cars from its reserve fleet; that made conditions worse. Its reservation system broke down, too, and often the same seat was sold to two persons.

Perhaps those who tried the trains again at that time were expecting too much. Some were delighted with their experience on certain trains; they had forgotten how nice it was to have so much room to move around while traveling and so much space for luggage, instead of sitting with elbows drawn tight on crowded airliners. Others had horror stories to tell about trains

163

Scores of modern new coaches have been added to the Amtrak fleet. This typical Amcoach of the Amfleet line seats 84 passengers in reclining seats with fold-down tables and armrests.

that arrived hours late and coaches in which seats were broken, the air conditioning or heating failed, windows were covered with mud, and trainmen were impolite.

Many coaches were so old that spare parts to repair them could be obtained only by removing them from other cars—"cannibalizing" equipment.

So many complaints were heard that the Interstate Commerce Commission held hearings at which Amtrak passengers were invited to tell their troubles. They had ample to tell. One family reported on a summertime trip from New Jersey to Florida during which the air conditioning broke down and they saw roaches on the dining car tables. The Amtrak personnel were so rude, the father testified, that passengers were afraid to ask for pillows. His wife's pillow was grabbed away from her in the morning by a train staff member who said, "Time's up." Another witness told of a revolt by passengers on a southbound East Coast train. Temperatures in the coaches were about ninety degrees, so hot that many passengers refused to travel beyond Richmond, Virginia. They forced the train to wait there an hour while they argued with Amtrak officials. Although most passengers eventually went back on board, some families did not.

On a famous-name train, the Panama Limited, from Chicago to New Orleans, a passenger described a trip during which the air conditioning collapsed; then the electricity in the cars failed completely. And on the James Whitcomb Riley, between Chicago and Washington, D.C., a witness testified that when he complained about the dirty cars and late service, an Amtrak conductor threatened to throw him off the train if he said anything more.

These were extreme examples. Not all Amtrak service was like that. Many people loved their trips, but even high officials of the organization admitted that often passengers received treatment they didn't deserve.

After awhile, the trains began to improve. Amtrak ordered hundreds of new coaches to replace the worn-out equipment it had inherited. Rude employees were replaced. A sense of pride in railroading was preached to the new Amtrak workers. They

Passengers seated on the upper level of dome cars have an especially good view. This picture was taken aboard the Amtrak San Francisco Zephyr.

The San Francisco Zephyr operated by Amtrak twists through mile-high Emigrant Gap in the High Sierras between Reno, Nevada, and Sacramento, California.

smiled, and the passengers smiled back at them. New locomotives were ordered for faster speeds. On some routes, especially in the West, Amtrak trains lived up to the finest traditions of railroading.

If the first Amtrak trains were in sorry condition, the tracks over which they ran were even worse. These tracks still belonged to the private railroads, not to Amtrak. In many instances, especially on the bankrupt Penn Central, the railroad companies ignored necessary repairs to their tracks even after Amtrak began. Instead of two ruler-straight lines of steel disappearing into the distance, rails warped by disintegrating wooden crossties and lack of ballast at times looked like free-hand squiggles drawn by a kindergartener on rough paper.

This meant that Amtrak didn't dare run its new trains at the speeds they were designed to go. "Slow orders" were sometimes so extreme that engineers on some runs could not operate their trains faster than ten miles an hour over long stretches. Even the Metroliners that touched 100 miles an hour didn't dare attempt the 125-mile-an-hour speeds for which they were designed. Sleek new French-built Turboliners on runs out of Chicago, also capable of 125 miles an hour, were ordered not to exceed 79 miles an hour. More than half of the Amtrak trains arrived late, as much as three hours on some runs, during the first years.

When the president of Amtrak, Paul H. Reistrup, rode one of his trains over badly neglected Penn Central track in Indiana, he told a reporter later, "Our train was going so slowly we were overtaken by a worm-laden robin."

Rebuilding track to proper condition was an even slower and more costly task than improving Amtrak equipment. On some lines the rebuilding was done with federal assistance under the plan by which Conrail, a government subsidized corporation, took over several bankrupt railroads in the Northeast, including Penn Central. Gradually Amtrak service improved. More trains reached their destinations on time. More passengers found themselves well treated, on pleasant coaches with relatively smooth rides. New routes were added, one by one.

The passengers were pleased to find surprises on some trains, too—pianos in lounge cars, balloons and hats for the children, and young women in place of the traditional male Pullman porters. The men who run Amtrak are trying to make train travel

French-built Turboliners are among the distinctive new types of equipment added to the Amtrak railroad fleet.

Train travel can be fun: The observation lounge car on the Super Chief; some games along the way; an Amtrak diner on the Florida run. Many Amtrak trains carry diners where tasty, substantial meals are served at reasonable prices.

appealing again. They are beginning to succeed, despite their difficulties. Trains cannot match airliners for speed, but those who believe in the saying that "getting there is half the fun" say that a train is a far better way to see the country than flying thirty thousand feet above it.

Tours by train around the United States are offered by travel organizations, some of them luxurious and some of them economical. These enable Americans and visiting foreigners to see conveniently the natural and man-made wonders of the country, with hotel accommodations and local sight-seeing bus tickets included at the cities visited. Or, of course, individuals and families can make arrangements on their own.

Auto trains to Florida are another recently developed way to travel by rail. One originates in Virginia, another in Louisville, Kentucky. The traveler rides in the passenger coach with meals and entertainment included in the price of his ticket, and sleeping accommodations if he desires, while his automobile is carried aboard the same train in a special storage car. When the train reaches its destination, the traveler leaves the train and finds his auto waiting.

Train travel is fun again.

13

CHATTANOOGA CHOO-CHOO

Would you like to spend the night in a railroad sleeping car decorated in the ornate style of the Gay Nineties? It still can be done. A family of travelers who step aboard a Pullman car on the track at the Chattanooga, Tennessee, railroad station find themselves in a fascinating setting of long-ago days. Brass beds and plush upholstery catch their eyes. When they go to bed, they hope for a sound night's sleep, just as millions of Pullman passengers have done for the past hundred years.

There is a difference, however. No *click* of rolling wheels across rail joints sounds a lullaby for these Pullman travelers. When they awaken the next morning and raise the curtains of their sleeping car, they find the same railroad scenery they saw when they pulled down the blinds at bedtime. Their line of Pullman cars hasn't moved an inch. Since the train has no locomotive, and the section of track on which it stands is only a few yards long, this isn't surprising.

The overnight passengers are in a special kind of railroad station—one at which no trains have arrived for years. These days it is called "Chattanooga Choo-Choo."

In earlier times, the large railroad station of the Southern Railroad at Chattanooga, with its lavish 85-foot-high waiting room ceiling, handled thousands of passengers and dozens of trains each day, coming and going between the Deep South and the

Once the Southern Railway station in Chattanooga, Tennessee, this classic structure now houses a restaurant, shops, and a nostalgic display of railroad equipment.

North. A catchy hit song about this hustle and bustle, "Chattanooga Choo-Choo," that appeared in the 1940's had millions of Americans singing and humming.

When passenger train travel dried up during the 1960's, hundreds of railroad stations like Chattanooga's were left almost abandoned, because so few trains came to them. The restaurants, barber shops, news stands and small stores inside these stations were forced to close for lack of business. Light bulbs burned out and were not replaced. Dust and debris collected in the corners. The callboards on which arrivals and departures of trains were posted went unused, still listing departure times of trains that no longer existed. Redcap porter service ceased and the remaining passengers had to struggle with their baggage unaided. Eventually, train service ended completely at many stations.

Although the abandoned stations often were gems of architectural design, or in some cases spectacular monstrosities, nobody seemed to care. They were ghosts in the hearts of our cities.

171

The thousands of railroad stations in the United States took many distinctive forms, including this Arabian-style structure at Opa-locka, Florida, in the Miami area.

Without trains at their platforms, these stations no longer had a reason to exist. They became empty shells, faded and neglected, built for a way of life that was vanishing.

That is what happened to Chattanooga's station. The last train pulled away from the station in August, 1970, ending passenger service. The terminal's doors were boarded shut. It appeared to be headed for the same dismal fate as other stations all over the country—sale to a wrecker, and demolition.

Fortunately, that didn't happen in Chattanooga. A group of businessmen purchased the station, spruced it up, and gave it new life. The lofty waiting room and the concourse area where passengers once walked to the train gates were transformed into gaily decorated restaurants. The baggage room and other areas were converted into shops whose wares include engineer's overalls and caps. An intricate model railroad runs in one room. Flower gardens bloom where some tracks were. On other tracks, train equipment from the glory days of railroading stands for

This room under the highest free-standing dome in the world once was the main waiting room of the Southern Railway station in Chattanooga, Tennessee. Now it houses a large restaurant.

A wood-burning steam locomotive stands next to an old-fashioned trolley car at the Chattanooga Choo-Choo. Visitors may inspect the locomotive and ride on the trolley.

This unusual motel room is in a converted railroad sleeping car on a track at the Chattanooga Choo-Choo.

visitors to inspect, including a wood-burning locomotive and a club car from the old Wabash Cannonball. A little electric trolley car tootles along a track from the terminal to a parking lot. And shiny Southern Railroad sleeping cars stand on some tracks, remodeled into unusual motel rooms on motionless wheels.

It's exciting and busy and nostalgic, giving visitors a glimpse of how railroading used to be. So many people swarm to see the Chattanooga Choo-Choo that on warm summer evenings long lines of ticket-holders wait their turn to dine in the station. More than a million persons came to the revived station in the first year it was reopened, and not one arrived by train.

Railroad stations once were among the most important buildings in every city. Those built in the late 1800's and early 1900's frequently were as ornate as the most elaborate churches or mansions of millionaires with turrets, spires, bronze and gold-leaf decorations, even stained-glass windows. Great chandeliers hanging from the high ceilings cast their light across the marble floors of the waiting rooms. "Cavernous" is a word often used to describe the big city stations, because their ceilings were so high and their open spaces so great.

Railroad experts have calculated that forty thousand railroad stations were built in the United States from 1850 to 1950, most of the biggest ones around the beginning of the twentieth century. Thousands of them, big and small, met the same fate that almost befell the Chattanooga station: abandoned, locked up, and ignored. Vandals broke into them and lit bonfires on their once shiny stone floors. Windows were smashed; copper sheathing was stripped off their roofs by thieves to be sold for salvage. The stations stood with grimy walls and broken sidewalks, dreary leftovers that nobody knew what to do about.

Many were torn down, often to make room for tall office buildings in the large cities. Their central locations made the land on which they stood extremely valuable. Among those demolished was the Illinois Central Gulf Railroad station on the Chicago lake front, with its clock tower rising ten stories high. On a memorable day in 1893, during the Columbian Exposition, more than 500,000 travelers used the station, the greatest single-day movement through a railroad station ever recorded.

Not all old stations have been allowed to decay or have been torn down. Ingenious new uses have been found for them in other cities besides Chattanooga. The rescue of more old stations is being considered as the campaign to restore colorful old buildings gains momentum around the United States.

The Mount Royal Station in Baltimore has become a studio and gallery for the Maryland Institute College of Art, its skylight providing splendid light for painters and designers. The stately Union Station in Washington, D.C., was converted into a National Visitors Center for the nation's Bicentennial celebration. In Lincoln, Nebraska, a station built in the style of a French chateau became a drive-in bank where computers stand near a pot-bellied stove and other relics of passenger-train days. The Rockland, Maine, city hall occupies the former depot there. At Cincinnati, the station became a school. Smaller stations have been made over into restaurants or gift shops, and in a little northern Wisconsin town that hasn't seen a passenger train for many years, the station was turned into a small winery, where wines are made from fruit picked in the neighborhood. In a less dramatic use than these, but a very practical one, the Union Station at South Bend, Indiana, became a foam rubber factory for a time.

Even the largest and most spectacular of all American stations, Grand Central Terminal in the heart of New York City, has been threatened by change. "Terminal" is its proper title, but almost everyone calls it "Station." When anyone thinks of railroad grandeur, Grand Central comes to mind. The vast space of its marble-floored concourse, illuminated by dust-specked light streaming down from lofty windows so large that they look like walls of glass, is reminiscent of European cathedrals.

In the prosperous years of passenger service, scores and scores of long-distance trains were constantly arriving and departing through a tunnel from the upper level of the two-tiered station. Every day, 550 trains entered and left Grand Central. More than five hundred persons debarked from the Twentieth Century Lim-

175

Sunlight from the high windows streams down into the concourse of Grand Central Terminal, New York City, in this old photo.

ited alone on busy mornings. "Meet me at the information booth in the center of the concourse" was, and still is, a popular instruction. On the lower level, down a ramp, commuters to and from the New York suburbs scurried through the gates of the suburban train tracks. Swarms of them went out onto bustling 42nd Street or through the underground passages to the subway entrances. Travelers followed other passageways to nearby hotels—all without having to go outside into the weather.

Grand Central was a symbol of New York life to people all over the country. In the 1940's it was the imaginary setting for a dramatic radio network show. Each program began with the announcer saying tensely:

"As a bullet seeks its target, shining rails in every part of our great nation are aimed at Grand Central Station, heart of the country's greatest city. Drawn by the magnetic force of the fantastic metropolis, day and night great trains rush toward the Hudson River . . . and then . . . *Grand Central Station!* . . . Crossroads of a million private lives."

That is how it was during the daytime hours—a constant surge of human figures across the concourse, passengers lining up at the long row of ticket windows, resting in the waiting room, browsing in the shops, eating in the renowned Oyster Bar. Cowboy actor Tom Mix once rode his horse Tony through the station; Tony's steel-shod hoofs slipped on the marble floor. And on a memorable day thirty years ago, thirty-five Los Angeles policemen drove their motorcycles from their train through the concourse with a thundering roar that almost shook the walls and made spectators cover their ears with their hands.

In the midnight hours when no trains were coming or going, and the crowds of the day slept at home or aboard trains, Grand Central's massive chambers were empty, almost dead. At 3:00 A.M. the terminal was so quiet that when a lone visitor walked through the concourse, his footsteps echoed. A few scrubwomen mopped the floors and a stranded passenger or two slept restlessly on the oak benches, waiting for the morning's first trains out.

Grand Central today has lost some but not all its glamour, crowds, and excitement. Only a few Amtrak long distance trains use it, compared to the large New York Central fleet of older days, but the commuter trains still do and in the rush hours passengers still run to squeeze through the gates to departing trains at the last second. At one long line of windows, OTB clerks now sell horse race betting tickets instead of train fares. The porters have almost vanished.

The property on which Grand Central stands, in the very center of midtown Manhattan, is so valuable that real estate investors saw a way to make large profits. They proposed to cover Grand Central with an office building rising fifty-five stories that would shut out the graceful terminal's natural light and bury it beneath a shaft of steel, glass and concrete, taking away its architectural beauty. Some promoters even proposed tearing it down. Committees of prominent citizens, realizing what Grand Central meant to New York, organized a fight to save it. The battle went on with words and court hearings, sentiment aligned on one side and profit on the other. In this case, for once, sentiment seemed to be the winner.

That wasn't true with New York's other famous terminal, Penn Station, on the west side of Manhattan. Its vaulted ceiling of glass and sweeping staircase were familiar to hundreds of thousands of travelers for decades. A great clock in the station was a rendezvous beneath which many lovers bid farewell during the wars and met for brief reunions when the servicemen were home on 48-hour leaves. Penn Station was torn down to make room for a new Madison Square Garden arena and offices. The trains still arrive there, underground, but the grandeur is gone. Passengers come and go through a small low-ceilinged waiting room, adequate but nothing more.

Whether they leave from new utilitarian stations or from the classic terminals of earlier days, more and better passenger trains are running today than for several years past. One of the richest American traditions has been saved. The cry of "All aboard!" still sends a tingle up the spines of first-time train riders and veterans of the rails, alike. It is a call to distant places whose magic, temporarily dimmed, is once more exercising its lure.

ACKNOWLEDGMENTS AND BIBLIOGRAPHY

Researching and writing a book such as this requires the use of many sources and the assistance of helpful individuals.

I wish to express appreciation particularly to Bill Warrick, a railroad enthusiast, and Julius Ivancsics of the South Bend *Tribune* for help in the collection of illustrations; to the staff of the South Bend Public Library for the use of old magazine and newspaper files; to the Coachella Valley Historical Society of Indio, California, for material about early transcontinental railroad travel; and to the public relations staffs of the Santa Fe, Union Pacific, Southern Pacific, Illinois Central Gulf, Burlington Northern, Chicago and North Western, and Baltimore and Ohio Railroads and Pullman Standard for textual and pictorial materials.

I found the following books, culled from the massive amount of material written about railroads, especially helpful:

The Story of American Railroads, by Stewart H. Holbrook (Crown Publishers, 1947)

Santa Fe, The Railroad That Built an Empire, by James Marshall (Random House, 1945)

One Hundred Years of American Railroading, by John W. Starr, Jr. (Dodd, Mead, 1928)

A Treasury of Railroad Folklore, edited by B. A. Botkin and Alvin F. Harlow (Crown Publishers, 1953)

Pioneer Railroad, The Story of the Chicago and North Western System, by Robert J. Casey and W. A. S. Douglas (Whittlesey House, 1948)

Mansion on Wheels, by Lucius Beebe (Howell-North, 1959)

Southern Pacific, by Neill C. Wilson and Frank J. Taylor (McGraw-Hill, 1952)

Abraham Lincoln, The War Years, by Carl Sandburg, Vol. 4 (Harcourt, Brace, 1939)

Slow Train to Yesterday, by Archie Robertson (Houghton, Mifflin, 1945)

Railroad Panorama, by A. C. Kalmbach (Kalmbach Publishing Co., Milwaukee, Wis., 1944)

The Western Maryland Railway Story, by Harold A. Williams (Western Maryland Railway Co., 1952)

The Americans at Home, by David Macrae (E. P. Dutton, 1952; originally published 1871)

Steel Trails, the Epic of the Railroads, by Martin D. Stevers (Minton, Balch, 1933)

The Road of the Century, by Alvin F. Harlow (Creative Age Press, 1947)

"Across the Plains," by Robert Louis Stevenson (from *Longman's Magazine,* 1883)

INDEX

ABOUT THE AUTHOR

PHIL AULT is a veteran newspaper editor in the United States and abroad. During World War II he was a war correspondent in North Africa and Iceland, and chief of the London bureau of United Press.

A graduate of De Pauw University, he began his career as a weekly newspaper reporter in Illinois. He worked as a correspondent and editor in Chicago and New York; later he was a newspaper executive in California, where he lived for twenty years. At present he is associate editor of the South Bend *Tribune*. He has written extensively about the West.

Phil Ault is the author of numerous books, including two college textbooks. Among those he has written for young adults is the prize-winning *This Is the Desert*, an anecdotal history of the Southwest desert, and *These Are the Great Lakes*.